FINANCE THE DREAM
CREATIVE FINANCING FOR CREATIVE PEOPLE

ROB TERREL with LYDIA PLANTAMURA

© 2021 Rob Terell All rights reserved. No part of this publication may be reproduced, distributed, or transmitted in any form or by any means, including photocopying, recording, or other electronic or mechanical methods, without the prior written permission of the publisher, except in the case of brief quotations embodied in critical reviews and certain other noncommercial uses permitted by copyright law. ISBN 978-1-66781-645-6

This book is dedicated to my brother David who is not here to witness the great things we're doing right now, but I know he is always with me in spirit cheering me on. Rest in Power lil bro! We got this! We're going to accomplish everything we talked and dreamed about when we were kids. To my kids Niles, Derek, Brock, and Madi....this book is another piece to our legacy!

Continue to dream beyond what you can see.

He who is not contented with what he has would not be contented with what he would like to have.

-Socrates

Many talented and gifted creatives have pursued their lifelong dreams of making it in the entertainment industry. The business is tough, cold, grimey, and gritty even if you're super talented. Talent is not enough, you need capital! Every creative needs a qualified team to help them reach that next level, in order to get experienced professionals working for you, you have to pay them. The daunting challenges inherent to the industry and efforts to build a viable brand seem to always intersect with the financial arena. The lack of any significant interest in financing independent creative ideas can become a dream killer.

Finance the Dream tackles the financial landscape that all creatives will inevitably face and provides practical advice and solutions that could be the difference between realizing the dream or the dream becoming a nightmare.

CONTENTS

Chapter 1
　The Situation 1
Chapter 2
　Creative Financing for Creative People 11
Chapter 3
　Mindset Reset 19
Chapter 4
　Give Yourself Some Credit 28
Chapter 5
　Solid Foundation 38
Chapter 6
　The Business of Business Credit 50
Chapter 7
　Find a Way… 64
Chapter 8
　What's The Score? 75
Chapter 9
　Private Investors 90
Chapter 10
　The Friends and Family Plan 97
Chapter 11
　Creative Hustle 105
Chapter 12
　Finance the Dream 113
Bonus Chapter 13
　The 9 Most Devastating Mistakes 121
Bonus Chapter 14
　Vital Questions You Must Ask
　Business Credit Building Companies! 129
Acknowledgments 133

CHAPTER 1

THE SITUATION

Passion.

This is where it starts. Creativity captures the heart and you must pursue it. Once a creative discovers what they want, the passion becomes the purpose. They start a grand mission of manifesting ideas into physical reality through the artistic medium of your choice. Perhaps you're a singer trying to connect to the world with the sound of your voice. Maybe you're a filmmaker hoping to share a story visually with a camera. You could be a model attempting to convey an entire mood in one striking pose. Whatever your medium, as a creative, you have a deep longing to express yourself. It grows, becoming a part of your essence. You define yourself by this passion and begin to view it as your calling and your true purpose.

A Hobbyist is Born.

Like a new relationship, at first, the love for art is exciting. Inspiration comes easily and you do it just for fun and the pure joy it brings. You are experimenting and learning new things. Your skills improve, and you are showing real talent. Soon, people start to take notice.

"Your music should be on Spotify playlists," friends and family say.

"You should open an Etsy store for your art," they encourage.

"Start a YouTube Channel!"

The Great Chase.

Different creatives are chasing different things. Some are truly chasing their passion and they could care less about the money. Some are chasing fame, others are chasing money, and a majority are chasing their passion or true purpose. Some are looking for all of the above.

The hard truth is that the entertainment industry is one of the hardest industries to "make it" in. Very few people chasing this dream will reach their desired end goal of fame and fortune. Oddly enough, a lot of creatives chasing this dream don't even recognize the unlikely chance of success. Competition is fierce with millions of others trying to break in too. You might be really, really good at what you do, but so are many other artists out there. The odds are stacked against you until you can compete on the same level as those who are already in the game.

As you embark on this journey, you start to learn about all of the additional things you never thought about before, all the things you need to level the playing field and help you stand out from the rest. You need decent film equipment to launch your YouTube channel. And a professional website to sell your merch. Plus, you'll need social media promotion to boost your following. You discover more and more things that you will need to pursue the creative career of your dreams. It builds up, reaching a point where it doesn't even matter how talented you are. Regardless of your craft and skill, these other necessities must be addressed for you to continue forward. You start to ask yourself, "Can I even afford to be a rapper?" "Can I even afford to be a painter?" "Can I even afford to be a comedian?"

No matter what your desire, no matter what you're pursuing, it's the great chase until you hit a financial wall that says, "You can't afford to chase the dream."

Critical Crossroads.

You've hit a fork in the road. There are two paths ahead. In one direction, you continue to view your passion as a hobby. It is simply something you do in your free time, just for fun. You don't want it to become work. In the other direction, though, your passion becomes a full-time career. It is your livelihood and creativity flows into your entire lifestyle. While the path

The Situation

toward hobbyist is free and clear, the road to becoming a full-time artist is treacherous. Some will try to rush hell with a squirt gun, but they all get burnt. Immediately you begin to see the biggest obstacle blocking your way to a creative career: money.

The Situation.

The further and further you get into your artistic pursuit, the more your expenses start to unravel. It incrementally increases along the way. Depending on what you do, it can start small but, for most artists, it won't be long before your needs outweigh your disposable income. For example, a rap artist might have no cost upfront to start writing bars, but soon they want to buy better beats. Then they need studio time and realize that comes with a cost for a professional engineer. They start paying a producer. Now they hire a manager. Next, they find a film crew to shoot music videos. Soon, they'll need marketing and promotion to build a following on social media. As they get bigger, they decide to hire a brand manager and PR specialist. None of this comes free and the list of needs continues to grow endlessly. Money is the elephant in the room.

The Ultimate Dilemma.

You have the talent, but you need funding to pursue it. Tens of thousands of dollars can stack up quickly in the entertainment industry. For some creatives, like filmmakers who need pricy equipment and entire crews on set, this number can easily add up to a budget in the millions for just one project.

You continue to ask yourself, "I have the dream, but can I afford to keep it?"

As the imminent financial situation grows, looming over the head of a creative, they come to an epiphany. Most people don't realize that the money will stop them. Their ideology says that talent is enough to carry them through, but the toughest lesson to learn in creative careers is that talent isn't enough. This part of the artist's journey is a huge dilemma, but an honest reality that must be faced.

Tension Builds.

An inner conflict is created between your desire and your financial situation. It is a dilemma. A total bummer. The harsh reality is, you still have rent and bills to pay. You have to put food on the table. You have basic living expenses that need to be paid. When money gets tight for the artist, it can be a devastating wake-up call. The fact of the matter is, at first, your passion isn't paying you. You are paying the passion. So how can you afford to live and be an artist at the same time?

For some reason, artists struggle to figure out all of the intricate details that tie into becoming a professional creative. They can figure out how to upload music to online streaming platforms. They can find open mic nights and opportunities to perform. They can teach themselves new techniques with their craft. When it comes to the financial aspect of their career, however, most creatives struggle. Rather than support themselves on the art, they turn to something more easily attainable. Most people go out and get a traditional job to make ends meet. They start waiting tables, or take third shift gigs, or work a 9 to 5, all of which siphon precious time away from the creative endeavor. Many will get stuck in their day job, trapped by the necessity to continue supporting their lifestyle.

Unwavering Faith.

Becoming a professional singer, dancer, designer, actor, filmmaker, model, comedian, etc. requires unwavering faith. You must have faith in yourself. You have to believe beyond belief that somehow, someway, something miraculous will happen and it will all work out. For a long time, though, you will feel like you are investing time, energy, and money into something that offers very little in return. At first, you will only be rewarded with personal benefits. Your reward is the joy that activity brings you by doing it.

You have to believe in yourself because for a very, very long time you are investing both time and money without seeing any payoff. It's disheartening and discouraging. The love for the art grows dull. What was once a

The Situation

passion has now become a chore. It's like being in a marriage and realizing that the passion is gone. You feel obligated to continue because the love is still there, but there is so much to maintain. Do you separate? Do you give up? What do you do? Creatives in this position feel lost. There are a lot of question marks, but very few answers.

The Rubber Band Effect.

The problem here is that the main job drains you. It takes energy away from what it is that you truly want to be doing. Some days, they find themselves too burned out to create. There is a lot of inner turmoil and emotional conflict building inside. This tension is constantly seeking to resolve itself. Imagine a rubber band you are holding between two hands. You can try pulling it in two opposite directions, but the harder you pull, the tighter it gets. If you keep straining the band, eventually, it's going to pop. That lingering pressure is building inside of the artist who wants to go pro. It's a conflict between settling for what is easy or striving to achieve your true calling. That tension continues to build, but it won't stay taught forever. Eventually, something will break.

Snap.

As the desire festers beneath the surface, the seed of doubt is planted, and new fears begin to sprout.

"Is this really my purpose?" you ask. "If it were meant to be, shouldn't it have happened by now?"

The passion feels heavy now. The pursuit becomes a daunting situation, dark and heavy, it weighs on your mental, spiritual, and emotional health. The spark you once felt fades and the fires of motivation grow cold.

The dream becomes a nightmare!

Depression and anxiety begin to sink in. You may lose friends. Family might turn their back on you while you run through different jobs, gigs, and schemes of making ends meet, all to continue funneling money into a creative project that just isn't coming together for you. After years of waiting for their big break, many are thirsty. Eagerly, they will try anything to make it. Everyone is willing to flip for the right price at the right time. People get desperate when they want something long enough. Women sell their bodies and men degrade themselves. Some might turn to drugs and alcohol. They are willing to sell their souls and sacrifice who they are for a leg-up or a foot in the door. All of this, in the name of money.

When the Worst gets Worse

Business savvy is important for creatives. You can be preyed upon by people in the industry if you aren't careful and don't have your wits about you. It is a predatory industry by nature. After 25 years in the music and entertainment industry, I have seen it all. Countless artists have been robbed, raped, finessed, and conned out of money. You have to be extremely careful about how you're moving and who you are moving with.

Several years ago, an artist came to me asking for help. She wanted to be a singer. On her journey, this girl found a big-time music executive from New York. After much research, she saw that the executive had worked with big names, mega superstars in the industry. His office was filled with impressive plaques. He knew people and had all the right connections. The girl decided to reach out to him and they began having video conference calls discussing how he could help her career.

The singer's mother was a retired school teacher and wanted to help. The music executive broke down the necessary expenses. The company wanted to fly the girl to New York and put her up in an apartment paid for in advance. They sent an itemized list of everything they would need. To help with these expenses, the mom took out a home equity line of credit for $150,000, which they wired to this executive. This massive sum was supposed to cover studio time, promotion, PR work, marketing, radio airplay, and more.

The Situation

On a huge leap of faith, the girl moved to the big apple. Her living expenses were taken care of and she was able to immerse herself in the creative work. The singer was finally dedicating herself to the dream. In New York, she was going to the studio and working hard at her craft, but nothing was happening. She scheduled a meeting with the executive to voice her concerns. In the meeting, however, he came on to her, trying to coerce her into sexual intercourse. She resisted and things got bad.

The mother and family flew their daughter back home, but by the time they tried to go after the music executive, he was gone. They couldn't find or locate him. All of their money was lost. Their house fell under foreclosure, the daughter got a traditional job, and the mother came out of retirement. They struggled, working and trying to save the house. By the time they came to me for help, there was nothing I could do. By the end of it, they didn't even have money for a lawyer to sue. It was an absolute horror story. I shudder to think about what would have happened if she had actually slept with him. Would it have ended differently? The situation easily could have turned out much worse.

Lessons Learned

The truth is, you have to take risks in the entertainment industry. With the right plan, however, the risk can be greatly minimized. One of the mistakes this family made was using their personal property as an investment. They also should not have given this music executive all of the money upfront. They could have given it to him in increments, allowing them to see where their money was going, and determine if it was a legitimate investment. By paying in increments, it would have incited the executive and his company to prove themselves, giving the family more time to monitor the relationship. They also could have given the money to a lawyer and created an escrow account. That would have set up the sum to be paid in smaller increments, like $3,000 to $4,000 at a time. This would have been a legally binding situation and the family's investment would have been protected. There should have been a very extensive contract with specific terms and conditions drawn up.

Although they had lots of evidence in writing through emails and texts, in the end, that was not enough.

When it comes to making a career out of something creative, it appears that the whole thing is a risk. If you don't have the education to handle these big financial decisions correctly, you can and will be taken advantage of. Remember, this is a predatory industry by nature. Historically, it is known as a monster. There are plenty of stories about artists like TLC, Tony Braxton, and even Prince who reveal this dark side of the entertainment industry. The moral of the story here is learning as much as possible about the risks you must take in this business to be successful.

The Path to Success.

The truth is, you don't have to struggle. There is a way to the other side. You must build a bridge by hand to get there. And that bridge is built on a strong financial foundation.

The following chapters are here to serve as a guide for you on your creative journey. They lay the groundwork for viewing your talent as a business opportunity and offer specific methods you can use to access the funding needed to pursue a creative career path. We are bringing to the forefront strategies to utilize financial information that has not been trickling down to the independent space. The tools we are giving you are already being used by professional artists all across the industry, and you can use them too!

For some reason, the majority of financial experts have never thought to tackle this topic before. Very few people have both the specialized industry knowledge and the financial wisdom essential to addressing the subject of business tactics in the entertainment space. Approaching it from a unique perspective, this book is making new connections between business finance and creative projects. Our goal is to help you find funds to propel you forward into whatever artistic endeavor you choose. We are providing guaranteed tactics anyone can utilize, and setting you up for success.

"Money is the elephant in the room."

CHAPTER 2

CREATIVE FINANCING FOR CREATIVE PEOPLE

As creative as artists are, for some reason, they get less creative when it comes to financing their dream. They need to dig deep into their creative space and become super innovative at finding ways to fund their projects and career. Understand that this is *your* dream. Overstand that *you* and you alone are responsible for it. If you try one method and it doesn't work, try again. Find another way. Try something different. Many people give up if their first attempt isn't a wild success. Just as with practice you get better at your craft, with practice, you'll get better at the financing. Some people need to be pushed up against a wall and watch their dream nearly slip through their hands before they get resourceful. They have to get desperate before they start getting creative.

We've discussed some of the expenses an artist might need to cover in their creative journey. This can start small with the basic equipment, tools, and materials you need to start creating, but it will quickly grow and expand as you explore your medium. Let's take an aspiring screenwriter and director for example. Their big dream is to make a feature-length movie. They've dabbled with making short films and shooting music videos for friends, and now they're ready to dive into that big picture. First, they update and rent high-quality equipment for their project so it looks professional. Then they find the perfect place to use as a setting, but those locations come with fees running in the thousands each day. They hire a crew and cast actors. Cast and crew get paid anywhere from $40 per hour to upwards of $400 per hour. Remember, these costs add up every single day of production and a feature-length movie might take months to film. Even after the director says, "That's a wrap!" on set, the movie isn't done yet. Post-production comes next with the need for editors and digital artists. The aspiring filmmaker also wants a good soundtrack and film score, so they pay a composer and buy the rights to any popular song they want to use. They aren't even filming anymore, but the expenses just keep coming. When the movie is finally finished, they'll need to pay fees when submitting their project to festivals. They land a distributor but learn they need more funding for marketing. All of these costs are upfront. They'll need to be paid before you get paid.

This is just one example, but it works similarly for any creative, whether you are working on dropping an album, writing a novel, or opening a gallery. There's also another layer to expenses that comes after the creation. Many artists overlook the expenses needed to promote their work. Without proper exposure, how will anyone even know that your project exists? To get your work in front of an audience of millions, you have to find a way to reach them. We advise designating at least 60-70% of your budget to marketing and promotion. Most creatives go the other way, investing only 20-30% of their funding into the business side of their work. It's easy to understand why. Artists live in the creative space. Their minds are absorbed with creating. They have a tunnel vision fixed only on making that final product perfect. They forget that there is one more step that comes after, and it is the most important part of the whole process.

A talented dancer-choreographer was trying to build her music career. She was a huge fan of entertainers like Janet Jackson and Sia, so she invested all of her savings into creating a music video as she imagined it should be. Pulling money out of her saving, the dancer scraped together $10,000 to invest in the project. She found elegant costumes, hired professional dancers, and incorporated impressive effects. She was emulating her idols, big-name artists with access to huge budgets. As she worked on the project, issues kept coming up. She found out she needed insurance. Problems arose with location fees. In the process, the dancer used every penny to make one epic video. She ended up going over her budget, but the result was impressive.

"Rob, you have to see this video," she said, coming to me for help. "Just watch the video. There's nothing like this out there."

I noticed the video only had a few hundred views at the time, a modest number to say the least. She was right, though. The video was amazing!

"We're going to blow up after this, right?" she asked, excited.

"Yeah," I said, reassuring her. I began outlining our next steps: "We're going to need $2,500 for promotional ads, and then $1,500 to get the song on Spotify playlists. We should get the single some radio spins too; digital radio is a good place to start. We'll need about $850 for that."

She was completely silent.

After a moment, she said, "But, Rob, I don't have the money for any of that."

"What?"

"Look at the video. That was my whole savings," she explained. "I already spent $10,000 making the video."

"How is anyone going to see this video?" I asked her. "How will anyone even know about it? If $10,000 was your budget, then you should've done the video for $2,000 and put the rest into marketing."

There is often a disconnect between the artist and the final steps of the creative process. This is a common mistake artists make. They exhaust their resources on one project with nothing left over. Artists get so caught up in manifesting their idea into a product, they never think about what comes after the creative work is done. What happens when you leave the studio with that fire track? What happens after you finish filming that impactful short film? What happens after you create that elaborate sculpture? Obsessed with making a vastly superior product, creatives can lose sight of the final and most essential step in the process: promotion.

The singer-dancer made an incredible music video that went nowhere. She was devastated. It became a "best-kept secret," that only she and her friends knew about. Artists tend to work in a creative bubble. There was no one there to reel the dancer in on her budget. She spent so much time, money, and energy trying to make her project look like a million bucks, she never stopped to think about what comes after. If this is something you are guilty of in your own work, we recommend finding someone to keep you in check. Make sure there is a money-minded person on your team to remind you of the budget and the bigger picture. Beware the artist who gets so engrossed in creation, that it never dawns on them that something comes after. Even when a creative finishes making their product, they still aren't done yet. In fact, they're only halfway there. Artists need to be able to finance the promotional phase too if they hope to reach an engaged audience.

It's expensive to be a professional creative. These business expenses will seem minuscule and random at first, but they unfold incrementally as your career grows. It's like quicksand, the more you move, the deeper and deeper it gets. How do you avoid sinking? Where does the money come from? How do you find funding?

In the following chapters, we will reveal the most effective ways creatives can acquire funding for their work. Let's briefly cover some of the options you have.

An obvious option is using the money you already have access to. Personal credit means buying things with your own credit. Some artists use their savings, take out home equity, or pawn their possessions. If you have excellent personal credit, you might be able to take out a loan from the bank, but more often than not, you will have a hard time convincing traditional lenders to give you money to release a rap album, shoot a romcom, or write a fantasy novel. A bigger issue with personally funding their own projects is that many creatives are in debt. It could be student loans, medical bills, or a mortgage. Whatever it is, they are strapped for cash. Even though they know it would benefit their career to invest in their art, they just can't make it happen.

When they're just getting started, many creatives reach out to their tribe. I call this, *The Friends and Family Plan*. By calling upon your trusted friends and encouraging family, you can find the financial support you need to get the ball rolling. Explain to them what your goals are and be specific with your needs. Remember, no amount of help is too small. You may be surprised at who will chip in and how much you can raise.

By asking others to invest in your dream, you are transferring that belief to others. You have to help them see the vision and convince them that what you are attempting is accomplishable. Successful artists visualize their dream and see the end goal as their destiny. If you are skilled at proving your potential to others, try approaching a *Private Investor*. A private investor is anyone with disposable income above their own needs. They are willing to funnel money into a creative project with the hope of seeing a return on their investment. They are financially minded individuals looking for ways to diversify their income streams. You'll need to get out and network to find the right person to pitch your ideas to. There are lots of different types of investors, however, very few are experienced with investing in entertainment. This rare breed of investor usually has a creative spark of their own or might already be involved in your industry.

There are other options to make money and sustain your creative career like crowdfunding, selling merch, or freelancing services, but none of these compare to our biggest recommendation for creatives: using Business Credit. Of all of the options we cover in this book, business credit is by far the one we recommend most. This method trumps all of them!

Business credit is different from your personal line of credit, but it works very similarly. When you use business credit, your business is acting as a separate legal entity. It has its own identification, similar to your social security number, called an Employer Identification Number, or EIN. With an EIN, your business can do things like open a bank account, apply for a credit card, and take out a bank loan. One of the reasons we love business credit is because business credit will grow with you over time. It is something you can utilize at any point in your career and provides you with full creative freedom.

While we strongly recommend business credit, it definitely isn't a quick and easy fix. It takes time to build a strong line of credit with your business, but if you give yourself five to ten years, you'll be set! There are a few things you can do to expedite that timeline, though. Assuming you've paid your debts on time, you can build your business credit up in a matter of years. With programs like the one offered by our company, World Capital Credit, you can speed through the process. Our course is affordable and convenient, offering all their classes online, so you can take it on your own time. It is a solid guarantee and if you follow all of the steps correctly, you can gain access to $25,000 - $50,000 of credit for your business in just six months to a year. https://worldcapitalcredit.com/

Whatever method you follow, remember that your dream is your responsibility. Funding is out there; you just have to get creative with how to find it. Building a financial foundation is crucial to the success of your artistic career. Do whatever you can to move the needle a bit and get things started. Once you have a solid financial basis to build on, you will tap into opportunities previously unavailable to you. The right funding will give you the ability to do so much more with your creative business.

"To get your work in front of an audience of millions, you have to find a way to reach them."

-Robert Terell

CHAPTER 3

MINDSET RESET

On your voyage of creative self-discovery, a moment of awakening must take place. Before we get into the nitty-gritty details about how to find funding, we need to take a moment to address mindset. If you only remember one thing from this book, let it be this: You are a business. You are a brand. As soon as you start profiting off of your creative products and services, then you are officially in business. Although your business is an entirely separate entity from yourself, you are ultimately responsible for it. Don't diminish your value by misunderstanding this. The right mindset will open up your whole financial universe.

When you choose the career path, your talent is no longer a hobby. There are responsibilities you have to fulfill to maintain the business. Artists who treat their work from a business perspective recognize that there are business expenses that come along with being a professional creative. The more you put into it, the more you'll get out of it. If you want it to pay you like a business, then you have to treat it like one. What they say is true, "It takes money to make money." When this finally dawns on creatives, they come to a stark realization: I need to invest in myself!

Taking your creative career seriously, be sure to establish yourself as a legitimate business. By putting everything under the business name, you create a layer of protection. When your company owns everything, it acts as a safety net. If any issues arise with legal altercations, you will be protected as an individual. If something happens to go wrong, the business will be held accountable and your individual line of credit and personal investments won't be affected. All successful artists have done this, and although many wealthy individuals have been sued, many of them have personal finances that remain unaffected because of this. By putting things under your business name, you have created a suit of armor. You cannot pierce the corporate veil to get to the individual. What this comes down to, is the power of control. Successful artists at the top of the game know this. Their business owns everything. They personally own nothing but control everything.

Let's break it down. As a creative, you are the business, the brand, and the product. Your creative projects or creative services are the product. Your brand is the voice, vibe, and essence of your business. And a business isn't a successful one unless you can invest in it and grow it. To be frank, nobody else will invest money in your dream if you aren't willing to invest in yourself. Investors want to see that there will be a return on their investment. The best way to demonstrate that is by first putting money into the business yourself and taking the first steps to prove it has value. Value is demonstrated by your profit margin, or how much you end up making after cost. In the digital age, value can also be demonstrated by your audience. To demonstrate, an artist with a large following on social media, or a musician with an impressive amount of subscribers, or a filmmaker with a massive number of views, would be considered a viable investment.

Engagement is also essential to building and establishing your brand. How are followers interacting with the content you are sharing? Does the project have a super high reaction? Or is it a moderate reaction? This can be frustrating for creatives when they start because, in the beginning, they will have a low reaction, and sometimes no reaction at all. These metrics all tie into the value of your project. It's not a hit until it's a hit, and ultimately, audience reaction will determine that. The reception of your work is one factor no one will know until you put the product out into the world of consumers. Your job is to put your product in the best possible position of exposure to allow the opportunity for a real "super" reaction to occur.

An artist's reach is the biggest value proposition. Most platforms have some threshold users must reach in order to be "verified" or to monetize an account. TikTok, for example, requires content creators to have 10,000 followers and 100,000 views on their videos in the last month. This is a good place to start. For anyone trying to break into the entertainment industry big time, your goal is to reach critical mass. Critical mass is anywhere between 25-100 million people in your audience. Anything less and it becomes a daunting task to make it to the highest levels of success. These are just examples of where you are trying to go. With direction, patience, and persistence you'll get there. Building a creative career is like climbing Mount Everest. The task at hand seems impossible at first, but it can be accomplished by focusing on taking one step at a time.

In the digital age, many creatives hope they will make it by going viral. The biggest misconception about going viral is that it is easy. People love to look at success stories, but very few people look at the failures. It's easy to talk about how many shots Michael Jordan has made in his career, but how many has he missed? No one wants to talk about this stuff. Think about it, you can point at 8 or 9 songs that went viral on TikTok this week, but what about the hundreds of thousands of songs that didn't go anywhere? If it were that easy, everybody would be making it big. There is an unrealistic view artist have of this concept. They live in a fantasy state, not realizing that going viral is like winning the lottery. This is the reality at hand. Going viral happens to one out of millions of people attempting to gain traction online. Don't let yourself get trapped in a dreamy headspace. The failure rate for going viral is enormous. It is not that going viral is impossible; it's just not probable. And it's not a solid business plan. With probability working against you, it's not something you can count on. It's chance versus probability.

Consider this: if your roommate told you that they weren't worried about paying rent next month because they've been buying lottery tickets all year and they're certain that they will win millions any day now, you would probably give them a sideways look. You wouldn't be very confident that your roommate would have rent, right? You would be concerned because it's not a viable plan. The same is true for creatives who are banking on having that one video go viral on TikTok. It is not a stable plan and there are better ways.

Putting their work out into the world for the first time is often a big wake-up call for creatives. Artists often have a skewed view of where they compare to other artists. They may be very talented and have a considerable following in their hometown, but if they are only reaching those in their community, then they are essentially a big fish in a small pond. Once they start putting their music out on the internet, however, they are suddenly competing with the entire world. They are not just a small fish in a big pond, they are a small fish in the freaking ocean! They are swimming with sharks and the competition is fierce!

For most creatives, their career is a marathon, not a sprint. Taking those early steps becomes difficult, though, when they approach the first financial hurdles they must overcome. Lack of capital hinders progress. Money becomes that elephant in the room. An artist might have everything lined up for their project. They've developed their craft, learned new skills, and met the right people to collaborate with. They are in love with their idea. But they hit a wall as soon as they realize they need money to invest in the project. They get stuck in the idea phase. The project gets put on hold. Wrapped up in their creative bubble, an artist struggles to see anything outside. They lack perspective. This is very frustrating for a creative because they don't understand why a team won't get behind them. After all, it's such a good idea!

Creatives dream of having someone so impressed with an idea that they just want to do it right off the bat. The problem is, your idea is your baby. You love it unconditionally and can easily see its full potential. Investors won't approach it with the same obsessive drive you have. They will struggle to see your end goal. You have to translate that belief in a way others will understand. You need to invest in yourself. Investors want to see that you have some skin in the game and that you have moved past the idea phase before they will get involved.

Imagine, a creative meets a potential investor.

"Oh! You're a singer," the investor says. "Well, can I hear a song?"

"Um, well, I haven't been able to record anything yet because I can't afford to get into the studio."

Notice how that will sound to an investor. You'll need to have something to show in the physical manifestation of the idea. Sure, it's a good concept, but what do you have to show for it? Any investor will have a hard time putting up money when there is no evidence that you will be able to deliver what you are trying to sell them on. Instead, if you have already invested in yourself and started moving toward your goal, you will have a much more compelling pitch.

"I'm already doing it," you can tell them. "I just want to do it on a larger scale."

This way, you are already making moves, you just need to rally people behind you to help push you further. This is much more appealing to an investor than someone who is still stuck in the conceptual stage of their project. Once you shift past the idea phase, you move into the business side of things. The finances act as a catalyst. I call this the business of music. Your career is a vehicle and the money puts gas in the tank. It helps the project move forward. You have to put your own gas into the tank to get things moving. Down the road, you might pick someone up along the way who puts gas in the tank for you. Maybe further along you pick up a bunch of people and someone in the car says, "Hey! It's getting cramped in here. Let's get a bigger vehicle." And they upgrade you to something even better. This is how the whole thing operates.

Artists are notoriously bad with finances. I've worked with so many creatives that are downright horrible with money. We argued about money all the time. Every week it was something else. In their minds, they have already made it. They assume that the money is always going to be there. Instead of viewing it as a business and paying themselves accordingly, they splurge, eager to reward themselves for how far they've come. They want the custom-made Versace outfit for the club today. They want a music video that makes them look like Jay-Z. They lease a Ferrari and give handouts to all their family, friends, and lovers. They make the mistake of thinking that there is an endless supply of funds. All it could take is one bad article, one negative media post, one poor review, and millions of dollars will literally dry up in minutes. Perhaps your hit is just a one-hit-wonder. Who knows, this could be your only moment in the spotlight. You have to build slowly and spend modestly. Increase your lifestyle gradually and proportionately.

A word of wisdom: Keeping up with the Joneses escalates quickly. It's not about how much money you make, it's about what you spend. Here's a thought, if I make 1 million dollars a year, but my lifestyle costs $999,990 to maintain, then how much money did I really earn that year? At the end of the year, all I have left for my work is ten dollars. Am I still a millionaire?

It's expensive to live a lavish lifestyle. Spend modestly with respect to what you are making. And never spend money before you get the check. Deals can fall apart. Creatives are often already off to the races before the ink is dry. It's okay to think positive and hope for the best, but always prepare for the worst. Don't be reckless with your funds. Artists have a habit of creating a lot of debt while they're still in the idea stage. They want to ball out, creating the illusion and perception that they are at a higher level than where they actually are. They miss appropriate funds to create the image of success. Disconnected from the reality of their financial situation, they feel a moment of arrival. The problem is, they are often faking it before they've made it. As Ice Cube put it, "Check yourself before you wreck yourself." You may have leveled up, but there are many more levels to the game. You aren't there yet.

If you struggle with this part of the creative business, then put someone on your team who is good with the finances. Find someone you trust and respect who knows how it all works. Having a financial advisor or business manager handling the money will keep you accountable and remind you of the budget. You want them to be there to reel you in when you get carried away on a project or stuck in your creative bubble. This person is an extremely valuable member of your team because they will give you more free time to focus on the art. Building a solid team to support you is another essential investment you will have to make to propel your career forward. Never underestimate the importance of those helping to make your dream a reality.

In the early stages of a creative career, you might find it hard to motivate others to get behind your dream. Think about it, though. Why should they help you? Unfortunately, most people want to be paid to put work in on someone else's dream. They aren't going to do it for free. Would you use your talent, time, and energy on someone else's project for free? No way! Not if you value yourself as a professional creative. The cold hard truth is nothing comes for free.

There's that elephant again. Money just keeps getting in the way. So many creatives struggle with their finances. When you get to the root of the problem, many of us are already programmed to think about money in a certain way. You may have to break the preconceived notions you have and start thinking about your finances differently. Most artists want to spend all of their time on what they create. That is where they live, in the art. They lose focus on the other factors that tie into their success. But as Robert T. Kiyosaki said in his book, "Money without financial intelligence is money soon gone." Most artists have to get to the point of necessity before they will take the time to learn business skills. Once they dig in, though, they are off on a wild journey down the rabbit hole of business finance.

"Most artists want to spend all of their time on what they create. That is where they live, in the art."

-Robert Terell

CHAPTER 4

GIVE YOURSELF SOME CREDIT

Welcome to the exciting world of business credit! Business credit is an important tool for any business, and can be extremely useful for obtaining funding and maximizing a business owner's borrowing power. So, what exactly is business credit? I'm so glad you asked...

WHAT IS BUSINESS CREDIT?

Credit is the ability to buy goods and services with an agreement to pay later. The simple definition of business credit is: Business credit is credit that is obtained in the name of a business.

Business Mindset

In the last chapter, we spent a lot of time focused on mindset. As we continue through the next few chapters, continue to think about yourself as a business and look for ways to apply these steps to your own artistic venture. Remember, if you want to profit off of your passion and art, you have to start thinking about it like a functioning business. You are an entrepreneur now and soon you will have established your very own creative business!

Using Credit

Most creatives don't even understand the personal consumer credit system. And many more don't know anything at all about the business credit system.

Let's start by debunking some common business credit myths and explain what can be learned from them.

Myth #1 - Business Credit is Just Like Personal Credit.

This sounds like it ought to be true, but it isn't. Sure, the credit systems are similar. But there are some major differences that can seriously affect your business. For starters, the consumer credit system has, both in court and in congressional testimony, been shown to be fairly anti-consumer. The system works against consumers in often. It is prone to errors and tends to resist the correction of any errors by consumers or their advocates. In one example, even after a credit bureau lost in court, they continued to refuse for months to remove incorrect information from the person's credit reports. The business credit system is different. It is not anti-business (or anti-consumer) and is less prone to errors. And when there are legitimate errors, it tends to be easier to correct them.

Myth #2 - It Doesn't Hurt to Use Personal Credit in Place of Business Credit

This is a problematic way of thinking that can lead to big problems down the road. Using personal credit for business purposes puts your personal credit at risk for the sake of your business. By doing so, you limit the resources available to you personally and to your business. The end result could be disastrous. Imagine when your business credit needs exceed your personal credit capacity. And then you need to use your personal credit and can't because it's tied up by your business. No matter how you spin it, in the end using your personal credit for business is a bad idea.

Myth #3 - Business Credit and Personal Credit Are Not Related

Using your personal credit for business use is a bad idea. But we can't 100% separate business credit and personal credit. Often, especially when starting out with business credit, a company owner must provide a personal guarantee for the business credit loan or line of credit. When providing a personal guarantee, the company extending credit will not only check your business credit. They will check your personal credit history. While the business account won't show up on your personal credit report, the personal guarantee could eventually affect your personal credit if the business fails to meet its obligations. Aim to avoid that scenario (and you can) with careful planning and smart use of business credit.

Understanding the Basics

Using business credit will start with legitimizing your creative business. This means establishing your creative business as a legal entity. Once you've done this, you can put EVERYTHING under the company name. In doing this, you've created a veil of protection. If anything happens to you personally, your company will be safe. You can also have multiple companies and multiple lines of credit. Through credit, you have access to REAL money that you can invest into yourself and whatever creative project you are currently working on. Your business can open a bank account, get a checkbook, and file for a credit card. To start, you'll need to go through the legal process and register with your state. It's a very simple and straightforward process. You'll create an LLC, S Corp, or something similar. A single-member LLC is probably the simplest way to get started, especially if you are the only one at your company in the beginning. You can file online, and be prepared to pay a fee. After you file, you will be issued a and EIN number. You are issued this from the IRS. Your EIN is the same number of digits as your social security number. It's a 9-digit number. This is kind of like your company's social security number. When a baby is born, you give it a name and they are issued a social security number. When a business is born, you give it a name, and it is given an EIN number. The EIN allows you to open a bank account under your business and apply for credit. Now begins the journey of building credit for your business.

This is an amazing thing if you look at its inception and what it eventually builds up to. The EIN allows you to do many of the things you wanted to do for yourself, but now you can do it specifically under your business name. Your business is now a separate legal entity from you. You still represent your company, so everything that happens to it is a direct result of your actions. As long as you use it responsibly, you will build good credit and improve upon it for your future career. Avoid going out and spending recklessly. Don't buy more than you can afford and put yourself in debt. Instead, purchase only what you need and pay it back quickly. Overtime, your lines of credit will grow. Look at this decision as an overarching decision. In 5 or 10 years, you'll still be in business with the ability to borrow massive amounts of money. Some businesses have earned credit lines worth millions of dollars! Imagine the possibilities!

Everything You Should Know About Your Corporate Credit

Let's get into more detail. When you apply for business financing there are three types of credit reviewed when your approval is under consideration.

Personal Credit

No matter what you have been told, Personal Credit always matters, unless it isn't under review. For example, when applying for business credit you can use your EIN to get approval. Then only provide your SSN on the application for identification purposes. When you do this, your personal credit isn't even looked at, nor is it used for the lending decision. This is about the only exception in the business funding space. All other funding types including advances look at and care about your personal credit. Yes, you can get approval for cash flow financing and merchant advances with bad credit. But your repayment terms won't be nearly as favorable as if you had good personal credit. SBA loans, conventional loans, most other long-term loans, and credit lines often demand good personal credit for approval. Collateral and asset type-based financing doesn't care about personal credit as much. This is if financing only looks at collateral for approval, not financing where collateral is necessary for approval.

Bank Credit

With Bank Credit, your bank rating is mostly based on the amount of money you keep in your bank account over the last 90 days.

The scores work out as follows.

- High 5: account balance of $70,000 – 99,999
- Mid 5: account balance of $40,000 – 69,999
- Low 5: balance of $10,000 – 39,000
- High 4: 7,000 – 9,999
- Mid 4: 4,000 – 6,999
- Low 4: 1,000 – 3,999

Business Credit

Business credit is credit in a business name which is linked to the business's EIN number. This is credit a business owner can get which is not linked to their SSN. When you build business credit correctly, the SSN isn't even on the application. This means there is no personal credit check to get this kind of EIN credit. When you apply for something like an auto loan, the lender pulls your personal credit. They do so using your name, address, and social security number. This information goes to the consumer credit reporting agencies. They give the lender a credit report with all the information they have on someone with a similar name, address, and SSN. With this type of credit, an inquiry is then put on your consumer credit report. Your report is used to make the lending decision. Plus, the credit you get is then reported to the consumer reporting agencies. When you apply for something like a business loan, the lender pulls your business credit. This is done using your name, address, and EIN number. This information is sent to the business credit reporting agencies. They supply to the lender a credit report with all the information they have relating to a business with a similar name, address, and EIN. With this type of credit an inquiry is put on your business credit report. Your business report is used to make the lending decision.

Important Note: when applying for financing and credit using your business credit, you should not supply your Social Security number on the application, even though it is requested. When you do this, no personal credit can be pulled because the lender can't pull your personal credit without your

SSN. This forces them to only pull your EIN credit as you supplied your EIN not your SSN. This means you get approval only on the merits of your business credit report. Your personal report isn't even reviewed. Note: for bank loans, you must supply your SSN (it's an anti-money laundering requirement). But you can make sure it's only used for identification purposes. Also, make certain you aren't providing a personal guarantee.

The 5 Cs of Business Credit

1. *Character*

Character is all about you. It's about your personal history, your stability, and how reliable you are. This variable is more subjective than the others. It is one of several reasons it is best to do business with a bank where you have built relationships with the people who work there. The lender may check your education, work history, personal income, and personal credit history. This is one area of business credit where relationships matter!

2. *Capital*

Capital is about how much you have invested in your business. Whether you are seeking a bank loan or a loan from a private investor, the lender will want to see you are heavily invested in your own business. In general, the more of your personal money invested in your business, the better it looks to potential lenders. After all, if you're not confident enough to invest in your business, why should they be?

3. *Capacity*

Capacity is about your ability to repay a loan per the terms. Cash flow, payment history, and the assets and resources of anyone providing a personal guarantee play a part.

4. *Collateral*

Collateral is something offered up as security for a loan. Anything from equipment to inventory to a home you own can be collateral. It may be easier to get approval for loans with collateral, and many loans will demand it. In some cases, the more that you can offer as collateral, the more likely you will get approval.

5. *Conditions*

Conditions may mean any number of things, some of which could be out of your control. The current economy, for instance, may play a role in your ability to get approval for a loan. Other things they may look at include your industry and its economic status, and the loan's purpose. If your industry is suffering and businesses in your industry are struggling, it could harm your ability to get approval. Some loan purposes are easier to get approval for than others, too. Loans for riskier purposes like new and unproven expansions are often less likely to get approval.

Business Credit Benefits

Imagine having the ability to access a good $50,000 for your next creative project. Your success as a creative business is based on your business credit profile and score. With a good business credit profile, you will have near unlimited borrowing power. Without a good business credit profile, it will be a difficult path to success with no access to working capital and funding. This is why almost all Fortune 500 companies use their business credit to secure funding. It's not that they need the money to operate. Successful companies use funding as leverage to grow their business.

Business Credit is the best kept secret in the entertainment industry. Over 90% of creatives know nothing about it or business credit scores. But when you discover what business credit can do for you and your business, you will be floored at how easy it is to get money and grow your business. With a strong business credit profile, lenders will lend you money based on your business credit, not personal credit. This is excellent. If you have personal credit issues as you can still qualify for funding. Even with exceptional personal credit, business credit gives you DOUBLE the borrowing power. You can get approval for much more money with your business credit than if you used your personal credit to qualify.

Another great benefit of business credit is you may not need to provide a personal guarantee for some of the funding you get. This means you can get approval with no personal liability. So, if you ever default, the creditor can't pursue personal assets like your home or personal bank accounts. Business credit adds more value to your business and gives your business credibility. Stakeholders, partners, lenders, even potential buyers of your business will see more value in your business if you have a strong business credit profile. Most importantly, by having a good business credit profile built you have security. It is much easier to work on large creative projects when working capital is easy to come by.

"Understand that this is your dream. Overstand that you and you alone are responsible for it."

CHAPTER 5

SOLID FOUNDATION

Setting the groundwork for a solid financial foundation is vital to the success of your creative journey. Over 95% of creative businesses fail within their first 5 years in business. Surveys have shown the main reason for their failure is a lack of capital to help sustain and grow the business. Many of those businesses were producing good revenue. But the revenue wasn't enough to keep the artist creating, help the business grow, and leave enough money for the creative to draw a salary.

Why Every Professional Creative Should Have Business Credit

When done right, a creative can get business credit without an SSN going on the application. This means there is no credit check of the business owner for approval. This also means that anyone with bad, even horrible personal credit can still get business credit approval. Business credit reports to business credit reporting agencies, not consumer reporting agencies. So as business credit is used it has no adverse impact on the owner's consumer credit. This means using the account, even over 30%, won't have any adverse impact on personal credit scores. And there are no inquiries on the personal credit when you apply for business credit as long as you don't supply your SSN. 30% of your total consumer credit score comes from utilization. If you use your personal credit to get credit cards for your business and you use those cards, you will lower your scores. Using more than 30% of your limit results in a score decrease. So, if your limit is $1,000, having a balance above $300 lowers your scores. This means 40% of your total score is damaged by applying and using the credit you get with your consumer scores. With true business credit, 0% of your score is affected. 10% of your total consumer credit score is from inquiries.

If you are using your personal credit to apply for business loans and credit, your scores will go down as a result of those inquiries. Plus, those inquiries can remain on your credit for an extended period of time, thereby affecting your ability to borrow more money. And some unsecured business lending sources won't even lend you money if you have two inquiries or more on your personal credit reports in six months. But with business credit, the credit doesn't report to the consumer agencies. Neither inquiries nor utilization have any effect on your consumer credit scores. This is one more reason every highly successful business has business credit.

Have you ever tried to secure money at the bank? If so, then you already know how hard it can be to get approval. If you ask most business owners, you will find only a very small percentage have successfully gotten conventional bank funding for their business. Most conventional lenders offer only SBA financing. This means to get funding; you must work with the lender and the SBA. For approval, you would need to supply business and personal financials, tax returns for the last 3 years, evidence of all collateral and assets the business owns, a resume for you and all the other business owners, a business plan, personal and business bank statements for the last year, and much more.

Most businesses can't supply these documents, or there is an issue with one or more of the documents, preventing approval. Once the business owner is turned down at their main bank, studies have shown that they rarely look anywhere else for funding. The business owner isn't lazy; they just don't know where to look outside of their bank for money for their business.

Don't be one of the 95% of creative businesses that end in financial ruin. There are steps you can take for your business, to ensure approval for business financing. Be a creative success story, not an epic failure.

Ensure Your Business Has a Credible Foundation

One of the most important things ways to make certain you can get money for your business is to set up your business credibly. There is a secret set of requirements all lenders have, which they use to determine your approval. Although lenders don't want you to know about these secret requirements, they most assuredly exist. Making sure you meet them will be crucial to ensuring your business can get business credit and funding.

First, make sure your business name and EIN number is correct on all your licensing, tax documents, bills, and other pertinent documents. If this information is even a little off, you can get a denial. Also make sure you have all proper state, county, city, and federal licensing required for your profession. If you are a contractor for example but don't have your contractor's license, you won't get approval. You must be properly licensed to get approval for money for your business. Your business will need a website and a professional email address. Without a website listed on your application, you won't be able to get funding. You also won't get approval with an email like partydude@yahoo.com. Instead, you must have a professional email address like info@yourcompany.com. A professional email address and website go a long way to establishing business credibility. These details are crucial to getting business funding.

Your business also needs a toll-free phone number to get financing from a lender. And your main office phone number must have a listing with 411 to get approval. One of the most common steps a lender will take to determine approval is to check if your number has a listing in 411. If you don't have a toll-free number, or if your number doesn't have a listing in 411, you won't get an approval.

Your business will need to be a real physical location. Most lenders seem to prefer nonresidential addresses. If you don't have a physical office now, investigate companies who offer you a "virtual address". This is an address where you can rent from them and get your mail. Also, be sure to use this address for your loan applications. This will bolster the perception that your office is in a big physical office, even though it isn't. For approval, you must list a real, physical business address on funding applications. Make certain your business is set up credibly for the best chance to get approval for funding.

Establishing Your Business Credibility

The perception lenders, vendors, and creditors have of your business is critical to your ability to build strong business credit. Before applying for business credit, a business must ensure it meets or exceeds all lender credibility standards. It is very important that you use your exact business legal name. Your full business name should include any recorded DBA filing you will be using. Ensure your business name is exactly the same on your corporation papers, licenses, and bank statements.

You can build business credit with almost any corporate entity type. If you truly want to separate business credit from personal credit your business must be a separate legal entity not a sole proprietor or partnership. You need to be a Corporation or an LLC to separate personal from business. Whether you have employees or not, your business entity must have a Federal Tax ID number (EIN). Just like you have a Social Security Number, your business has an EIN. Your Tax ID number is used to open your bank account and to build your business credit profile.

It's actually not hard to build business credit. You just need to know the proper steps to get started. Business credit building isn't that much different than consumer credit. You start off with no credit established. You then get approval for new credit that reports to the BUSINESS credit reporting agencies helping you establish and initial credit profile and score. Once your profile and score are established, you can then use that profile to start getting more and more credit. As you grow your credit you will get access to more useful credit such as store credit cards and cash accounts such as Visa and MasterCard credit you can use anywhere. Your credit limits will also grow, so you'll have access to more and more credit as you continue to expand your credit profile. Let's jump in a take a look at the actual business credit building steps.

Be sure to verify that all agencies, banks, and trade credit vendors have your business listed with the same Tax ID number. Business Address must be a real brick and mortar building, deliverable physical address, preferably not a home address. It cannot be a PO Box and cannot be a UPS address. Some lenders will not approve and fund unless these criteria are met. You must have a dedicated business phone number that is listed with 411 directory assistance, under the business name. Lenders, vendors, creditors, and even insurance providers will verify that your business is listed with 411. A toll-free number will give your business credibility, but you must have a LOCAL business number for the listing with 411 directory assistance. Lenders perceive 800 Number or toll-free phone numbers as a sign of business credibility. Even if you're a single owner with a homebased business, a toll-free number provides the perception that you are an even bigger company. It's easy and inexpensive to set up a virtual local phone number or a toll free 800 number. A cell or home phone number as your main business line could get you flagged as an unestablished business that is too high of a risk. DON'T give a personal cell phone or residential phone as the business phone number. You can forward a virtual number to any cell or land line phone number.

Credit providers will research your company on the internet. It is best if they learned everything straight from your company website. Not having a company website will cripple your chances of getting business credit. There are many places online offering affordable business websites so you can have an internet presence that displays an overview of your company's services and contact information. It is important to get a company email address for your business. It's not only professional, but greatly helps your chances of getting the thumbs up from a credit provider. Setting up a business email address is just too easy and inexpensive to neglect.

One of the most common mistakes when building credit for your company is nonmatching business addresses on your business licenses. This is for reporting. Plus, you need to have the required licenses for your type of business to operate legally. You will need to contact the State, County, and City Government offices to see if there are any required licenses and permits to operate your type of business. You must have correct listings for state business, county license and/or permit, city license and/or permit and IRS filings. Take the time to verify that main agencies (State, IRS, Bank, and 411 national directory) have your business listed the same way and with your Exact Legal Name. Also take the time to ensure every bill you get (power bill, phone bill, landlord, etc.) has the business name listed right and comes to the business

Ensure You've Taken The Right Steps to Build Business Credit

Every highly successful business in this country has business credit. Most of these companies used their business credit to get as big as they are today. But contrary to what many believe, business credit is not only for big companies. Any company can build business credit! Big companies are often the ones that enjoy the benefits of business credit the most. This is because they have CFOs who know how to get and use business credit, whereas most small businesses don't. But you can get your hands on the exact same credit these larger companies have, if you know the formula to get it.

Get vendor credit immediately, starting now. It takes those accounts 30 – 90 days to report, giving you a profile and score. With that profile and score you can then start getting retail credit. And in a total of about 4 – 6 months after starting the process, then you can start to get cash credit. 90% of vendors in this country do not report the credit they issue you. This is why so many business owners think they have established business credit when they do not. So you must find vendors which report to the business credit reporting agencies. This is the hardest and most challenging part of building business credit. But once you get past this major hurdle, it's much easier to take the rest of the steps to get corporate credit. You must start a business credit profile and score with starter vendors. Starter vendors are ones which will give you initial credit even if you have no credit, no score, or no tradelines when you apply. Most retailers like Staples will not give you initial starter credit. So don't even try applying.

Building business credit can be as simple as finding the credit you want, applying with no SSN, and getting approval. Then start using your credit and pay your bills early. If you follow the steps, you should be well on your way with establishing business credit.

Step 1: Get Vendor Accounts

When establishing business credit, there are three types of credit you can get:

- Vendor credit, starter accounts that offer Net 30 terms.
- Retail credit, revolving credit cards available in retail stores.
- Cash credit, revolving credit cards like Visa and MasterCard. Card issuers or banks approve you for these.

You start with vendor credit or starter accounts offering Net 30 terms. Then you move onto retail credit. These are revolving credit cards available in retail stores. Finally, you get cash credit. These are revolving credit cards like Visa and MasterCard.

The biggest mistake entrepreneurs make when building business credit is that they try to apply for retail or cash credit first, and skip vendor credit. But retailers and banks will not approve a business owner for credit until their EIN credit profile and score are established. If you try to apply for retail or cash credit without an established business credit profile and score, you get a denial 100% of the time. You must get approval with vendors first which offer Net 30 terms. Then after you use those accounts and pay your bills, the accounts are reported to the business credit reporting agencies. Then and only then do you have an established business credit profile and score.

Once your business credit is established, you can start to get approval for retail revolving credit next. Seek out vendors which approve a business for credit, even if none is built yet. There are many vendor sources which are well known for this: Uline, Quill, Reliable, and Laughlin and Associates, just to name a few. Check out some real starter vendors. Quill Office Supplies offers office, packaging, and cleaning supplies. Their business credit account reports to Dun & Bradstreet. To get approval, place an initial order of $50 or more, unless your D&B score is already established. You may need to submit 2 – 3 orders before getting the Net 30 account. But make sure to apply first to either get approval or a decline. Then only if you get a decline should you pay for the order, then try again following the same steps. Uline Shipping Supplies sells shipping, packing, and industrial supplies. They report to D&B. You must have your D-U-N-S number. They will ask for two references and a bank reference. For the first few orders you might need to prepay to initially get approval for Net 30 terms.

To start business credit, get approval for accounts with these vendors. Some make you buy their products first. Some have you make three orders and pay before they issue you a line of credit. But all the sources listed will approve a brand-new business, even if you have no credit at the time you apply. You must have a total of five payment experiences reported before you even think of applying for retail credit. A payment experience is the reporting of an account to a business reporting agency. Quill, for example, reports to both D&B and Experian. That means that one account counts as two payment experiences. Laughlin only reports to Experian, counting as one payment experience. Once you have five payment experiences reporting, start to secure revolving retail credit cards for your EIN. Keep in mind: all applications ask for your Social Security Number.

But you do not need to provide your SSN on the application. If you supply your SSN, they will pull your personal credit. And if it's bad, you get a denial. When you leave the SSN field blank, they'll pull your business credit. And once they see that you have business credit established and at least five payment experiences reporting, you start to get approval for retail credit.

Make Sure You Monitor Your Payment Experiences

Building business credit is all about tradelines, or what are called payment experiences. A payment experience is the reporting of an account to a business credit bureau. So if an account reports to Dun & Bradstreet and Experian, it counts as two payments experiences. But if an account only reports to Experian, it only counts as one payment experience. To effectively build business credit you must be able to monitor your business credit reports to see these payment experiences being added. When you see this, you know when it's time to apply for more credit to build your credit profile and score. For example, you need five payment experiences before getting revolving retail credit like Dell, Best Buy, and Amazon. Monitor your credit so you know when you have five reporting. You should be monitoring your credit through Experian and D&B. You can go to their sites directly to enroll for credit monitoring.

Step 2: Retail Credit Cards

Once you have five vendor accounts reporting to the business credit reporting agencies, next you can start to secure revolving retail credit cards for your EIN. Most major retailers offer business as well as consumer credit. Staples, Office Depot, Home Depot, Lowes, Target, Walmart, Costco, Sam's Club, Radio Shack, Best Buy, BP, Chevron, Amazon, Shell, and most other retailers offer business credit. Some sources like Home Depot might have more stringent approval requirements. They may want to see big revenue and three years in business for approval with no personal guarantee credit. But most sources don't have these requirements, if you have business credit established.

WARNING!!!

Do not put your SSN on the application. Do not apply for revolving retail credit without at least five payment experiences reporting to the business credit reporting agencies. If you do either of these, you get a denial, or will have to give them your personal guarantee. Keep in mind: all applications ask for your SSN. But you do not need to provide your SSN on the application. If you supply your SSN, they will pull your personal credit and if it's bad you will get a denial. Leave the SSN field blank, and they'll pull your business credit. Once they see that you have business credit and at least five payment experiences, you start to get approval for retail credit. Most retailers will give you no PG credit, IF you have your business credit established. The key is to have a credit profile and score established. Otherwise, you won't get approval for 'no personal guarantee' credit at retailers or with banks.

A PG is needed when credit isn't established. But once it is, you can get approval with most sources regardless of your size or time in business, with a few exceptions. Now you're starting to uncover the secret formula for business credit building.

So let's revisit what not to do.

- Don't apply for retail credit first, you'll get a denial
- Don't start with cash or bank credit first, you'll get a denial
- Don't put your SSN on the application to start your business credit building. If you do, they'll pull your personal credit and demand a personal guarantee

Setting yourself up for success is an essential move in the creative business game. If artists take the time to learn the process correctly and follow the steps we offer, the result is an unbreakable ability to access funding for their future creative projects. While working with a hip-hop artist based in LA, I recommended he take our course at World Capital Credit. Living in the big city is expensive, and he was starting to run out of money. He took the last of his savings and invested it into his business education. He took our class and ended up with about $18,000-$19,000 worth of business credit. He was able to stay in the city and used the capital to put out his next record. His next record, ladies and gentlemen, landed attention from a few record labels, and he ended up signing a deal with an independent label. In this situation, business credit enabled him to make bigger moves with his career and grow to a higher elevation in the industry.

"Business credit enables creatives to make big moves with their career and grow to a higher elevation in the industry."

CHAPTER 6

THE BUSINESS OF BUSINESS CREDIT

Starting from scratch, how do you build business credit? Having access to money and credit for your creative venture ultimately determines your success or failure. A good business credit profile and score can be the difference between having a prosperous creative career or being at the helm of a sinking ship. You need money and credit to grow, especially to grow into a highly successful brand. This is one commonality ALL successful business have: established business credit.

Facebook, Microsoft, Apple, and every highly successful private and public company has business credit. The business can use its own credit profile to grow, without the owner or CEO providing personal credit or liability to secure that credit. Walmart gets 80% of their total cash injection from business credit alone. This is one of the reasons they have grown into one of the largest retailers in the world.

There are a ton of benefits that business credit provides. You can build a credit profile for a business that is completely separate from you the owner's personal credit profile. This gives business owners DOUBLE the borrowing power as they have both Personal and Business credit profiles. Business credit scores are based only on whether the business pays its bills on time. A business owner can get credit much faster using their business credit profile versus their personal credit profile. Approval limits are much higher on business accounts versus personal accounts.

Per SBA, credit limits on business cards are often 10 – 100 times higher than consumer credit. When done right, you can build Business Credit without a personal credit check. You can get business credit quickly, regardless of personal credit quality. Business credit doesn't report to the consumer credit reporting agencies and won't show up on your personal credit report.

As you get new business credit and use it, your scores won't plummet as they will with consumer credit. You can also get most business credit without the owner taking on personal liability, or a personal guarantee. This means in case of default; the business owner's personal assets can't be pursued. Even though most don't know this, when a business owner applies for financing, their business credit IS reviewed. Not having business credit established will get an owner DECLINED for financing. There are no regulations making lenders notify the business owner of their reason for denial. So most never know. The business can use its credit to qualify for revolving store credit cards. The business can also qualify for credit lines and loans.

Getting Your Business Credit Reports

Experian, Dun & Bradstreet, and Equifax offer business credit reports. You will first want to get a copy of your business credit reports to see what is being reported before you start your business credit building. We've made this easy for you by putting link for all business credit reporting agencies in one place. We even have affiliate relationships with them so they'll provide you with discounted pricing you won't normally find on your own.

You won't need to get reports with all three reporting agencies, but you should at least have monitoring set up with Dun & Bradstreet, and possibly Experian. With these reports you can find out how many trade lines are reporting, see if you have a business credit score assigned, see if you have an active Experian Business Profile, and check on recent inquiries. It can take more time to create a file with Equifax Small Business than D&B and Experian. This is because not a lot of vendors and creditors report to Equifax. Most report to Experian or D&B. This is also why it's important to apply with the credit providers who report to Equifax when you find them.

Dun & Bradstreet offer a CreditMonitor product where you can get unlimited access to your D&B reports and scores for a fee.

Getting Vendor Credit

When you started building your consumer credit report you probably did so with small limit credit cards, possibly even secure credit cards. A business credit report can be started much the same as a consumer report often is, with small credit cards, but in the business world these aren't secure credit cards, they just have set repayment terms versus being open ended revolving accounts. Your business can get approval for small credit cards to help you build an initial credit profile. These types of initial cards in the business world are often called vendor credit. You must start a business credit profile and score with starter vendors. Starter vendors are ones who will give you initial credit even if you have no credit, no score, or no tradelines (or what's called payment experiences now).

Most stores like Staples will NOT give you initial starter credit so DON'T even try applying. Most stores will NOT approve a business owner for business credit unless the owner has an established credit profile and score, just like in the consumer world. Vendor accounts must be used first to establish a profile and score, and then you can get store credit. It often takes 90 days or less to establish a score and profile with trade lines. A vendor line of credit is when a company (vendor) extends a line of credit to your business on Net 15, 30, 60 or 90 day terms. This means that you can buy their products or services up to a maximum dollar amount and you have 15, 30, 60 or 90 days to pay the bill in full. If you're set up on Net 30 terms and buy $300 worth of goods today, then that $300 is due within the next 30 days.

IMPORTANT NOTE:

If you do get set up for this you might get a call from Dun & Bradstreet Credibility. Keep in mind this is not Dun & Bradstreet; it is a completely separate privately owned company. Do NOT purchase their credit builder program no matter what they tell you. This is NOT something you need and NOT something you should pay for. This program only adds trade references to your report, but instead you should be building your business credit using real useable credit.

Always apply first without using your SSN. Some vendors will request it and some will even tell you on the phone they need to have it but submit first without it. Most credit issuers will approve you without your SSN if your EIN credit is strong enough. If your EIN credit is not good enough, you might be declined and they then might ask for your SSN. No matter what ANY credit representative tells you, you CAN get credit based on your EIN only. In the consumer credit world, we call these types of starter accounts as tradelines, but in the business world they are called payment experiences. A payment experience is the reporting of an account to one credit reporting agency. Some vendors require an initial prepaid order before they can approve your business for terms. Some companies like Uline might even require you buy from them 3 times for them to extend you credit, if you have no credit established now. All starters vendors have different requirements to approve you, but they are great sources to help you build initial business credit when you have none established now.

Getting Revolving Credit

After getting 3 vendor accounts, you can get revolving credit. Revolving accounts are cards a business owner can use and not be required to pay the full balance owed each month. Revolving account approvals will begin coming from stores. Get store revolving credit before getting Visa and MC type cards. Most stores will NOT approve a business owner for business credit unless the owner has an established credit profile and score just like in the consumer world. Starter vendor accounts must be used first to establish a profile and score, then you can get store credit. It usually takes only 90 days or less to establish a score and profile with trade lines.

Most major retail stores offer business credit accounts, although they don't promote that they do. And most of these retailers will approve you for new credit once you have a credit profile established, have a good business credit score from paying your bills as agreed, and once you have 3 accounts or more established on your business credit profile. Once 10 total accounts are on the credit, an owner can then start applying for Visa and MC type credit. Approval amounts will equal the highest credit limit account on the business report. Try to have 10 accounts with at least one of them having a $10,000 high limit. Keep using the credit and keep applying for more. Talk with credit providers to raise credit limits. Then business credit will keep growing until you get higher limit credit lines, within 6 – 12 months.

Building business credit is as easy as building consumer credit once you know the proper steps to take. Now you know the 4 essential steps to take to build business credit that's linked to your EIN and not your SSN. Now the next step is to act on the first step and make sure your business is set up credibly. As you do this get your business credit report access established. Then you can start building your vendor credit to establish your credit profile and score so you can start securing revolving credit accounts.

Many people ask, "how long does it take to build business credit?" Like with your consumer credit this is a never-ending process. You will always be growing your business credit as your business grows because you'll need to access more and more credit. If you pull a credit report for Walmart, you will find that their highest reported credit line has a limit of $50,000,000! But they didn't start out with those high of credit limits. They grew their credit over the course of 40 years. You may never need a credit line for $50,000,000. But as your company grows you will have an appetite for more and more credit. For this reason, building your business credit never stops. You can start getting vendor credit right away. It will take about 30 – 90 days for that new credit to report. So, it's a great time to apply for revolving store credit cards. Keep going with growing your credit! Get started today securing your first vendor accounts. This will net you a business credit profile and score you can then use to get real usable store credit. This leads to getting cash credit to help your business grow.

Build your Business Credit to Secure More Money

Lenders will review your business credit to determine approval. If you have a strong business credit profile and score, you have a much better chance of getting approval. If you have no to little business credit, you might not get an approval or may get smaller loans. Take steps to focus on building a business credit profile and score for your business. This will help you get approval, and help you get even more money. With business credit built, you can have double the borrowing power. This is because you can get credit as a consumer, and for your business. Plus you can easily build a solid business credit profile and score within only a year. And once built you can qualify for $100,000 or more in credit with no liability. Start by visiting Equifax, Experian, and Dun & Bradstreet. Get copies of your business credit report. Next, find 5 vendors to give you credit and report to the business credit reporting agencies. Once you use those accounts, pay them as agreed. When they are reported, you will then have a good business credit profile and score built. You can start getting approval for larger amounts of credit.

Factors That Affect Your Business Credit

What makes up your business credit score? What gives you the best chances of getting a loan? Here are a few factors that play into your business credit picture, and how you can make the most of them:

- *Payment History*

This is an important part of your business credit profile. It is the basis of your D&B PAYDEX score. Vendors will look at your whole credit picture and your PAYDEX is a part of that.

- *Blanket UCC Filings*

Pay attention to the order in which you get certain types of loans, and which UCC filings the lenders will file. Some lenders may file a blanket UCC filing. This essentially says they have an interest in ALL your assets. These blanket UCC filings will then take precedence over any later ones. This drastically reduces your ability to get credit elsewhere

What you can do: plan your credit with care and negotiate UCC filings according to your needs. For example, if you need particular assets excluded from a UCC filing to use as security for another loan, explain that in advance. That way, you can get those items excluded from any blanket filings. Or get the loan or account with the more specific UCC filing first. Some experts recommend opening accounts with competing UCC filings at the same time. And negotiate the details with each party simultaneously.

- *Company Financials*

With D&B, it's important to make sure your financials in your credit file are up to date. If they are not, it could negatively reflect on your company when the lender compares available data.

What you can do: update your financials on your credit reports. Make sure they reflect your current circumstances. And plan to update often.

- *Company Legal Structure*

Having an LLC or corporation versus partnership, etc. can also affect business credit. Lenders are less likely to loan money to sole proprietorships and partnerships. They prefer corporations and limited liability companies. So, if you aren't incorporated, you should be. The advantages go far past your ability to get credit. There are other factors affecting your ability to get credit, like the amount of debt you already have, and how heavily invested you are in your company.

Even your personal credit can play a role in your approval or denial. Here we've covered a few of them. The better the all-around picture you can paint, the better your chances of getting loan approvals.

6 Stages to Building Business Credit

Stage 1 - Set The Foundation For Building Business Credit

This foundational stage is all about establishing credibility for your company. Think about it from a lender's perspective. They are in business to lend to companies they consider to be safe risks. They perform several underwriting checks to see if you are safe enough for them to consider extending credit. Part of establishing yourself as a safe risk starts by being in compliance. Being in compliance helps you establish credibility for your company. This is foundational to your success!

Next, make sure your business is ready to build Business Credit. Define your business entity structure. As you build strong business credit, seek to protect it. Set up a business location and make sure your business is listed in 411 Directory Assistance for approval. Register for your business as an LLC or similar. Then get your EIN. You must verify that all of your agency listings are exactly the same.

Stage 2 – Optimize Banking, Assets and Revenue To Maximize Fundability

Stage 2 is all about business fundability. How fundable is your business? Fundability is about more than your business credit. It includes several components which determine how lenders, investors, insurers, suppliers, and more see your business. We know your business was worth the risk for you, but is it worth the risk for them? The answer will increasingly be "yes" as business fundability grows. By improving your business fundability, our Business Credit Building System goes beyond helping you build strong business credit. We improve the health of your business while greatly increasing your ability to succeed now and in the future.

The major components of Business Fundability are:

- Business Bank Accounts
- Business Assets
- Business Revenue
- The Owners and Their Credit History

Fund • a • bil • i • ty [adj. Fuhnd-uh-bil-i-tee]

You won't find Fundability on Dictionary.com, so don't bother looking. Fundability is a word coined to describe how a business measures up.

This is in relation to the entire business lending and investing community. Bank accounts are a vital business credit building component. Identify your business assets and availability for credit use. For the first round of funding, options are available. These are both with and without requiring a personal guarantee. A creatives personal credit can play a key role in building business credit.

Stage 3 – Get Set Up With All Three Business Credit Reporting Agencies

Stage 3 is all about the business credit reporting agencies. In Stage 3, we show you how to open and kick off your business credit files. This is with all three business credit reporting agencies. They are: Dun & Bradstreet, Experian, and Equifax. Most vendors use Dun & Bradstreet to extend lines of credit. Landlords use them to approve office leases as well. Many credit card companies and nontraditional business lenders use Experian. Equifax has the Small Business Financial Exchange. It is most important for cash lenders such as banks. To concentrate on one and not the others creates lopsided credibility. You need to build all three.

The how-to instructions in this stage clarify how to get started the right way with each Business Credit Reporting Agency. These methods have been tested and proven by thousands of our business members before you. There are some confusing claims made by the business credit reporting agencies. For instance, Dun & Bradstreet claims you must pay them or they will never open a business file for you. This is simply not true. Your file will activate with them, but it takes a few reporting cycles. Equifax claims they don't allow business owners to buy a copy of their reports. This is true, but we show how to get a copy of your Equifax business report without buying it.

Stage 4 – Starter Vendor Credit

Stage 4 is all about vendor credit. A vendor line of credit is when a company (vendor) extends a line of credit to your business on Net 30, 60 or 90 day terms. This means you can buy their products or services up to a certain dollar amount. And you have 30, 60 or 90 days to pay the bill in full. If you buy $300 worth of goods today, then the $300 is due within the next 30 days.

Some facts about vendor credit lines: You can get products and services your business needs and defer payment on those for 30 days. It thereby eases cash flow. This is Net 30. Many of our vendors open a Net 30 terms account with your company. And they will do so with as little as an EIN number and a verified 411 listing.

Start with our preferred vendor list. They are known to grant credit to companies with no credit history. Always apply first without your SSN; some vendors request it. Some even tell you on the phone they have to have it. Submit first without it, with your EIN only. If they ask you to personal guarantee it after you have submitted it without, then this is up to you. Some vendors may ask you to place an initial prepaid order. If so, get that order out of the way fast and move onto getting a Net 30 account for your second or third order. Remember, the goal here is to have at least five (5) Net 30 accounts open and reporting. Be patient. Allow time for vendor reporting cycles to get into the system and start impacting your business credit scores. It typically takes three (3) cycles of Net accounts reporting to build credit scores. In other words, it can take 60 to 90 days to get them to report and show up on your file. This is why it takes 90 to 120 days to build business credit scores. The credit reporting cycles are the main reason for this. It cannot happen any faster.

Stage 5 - Retail Credit

Stage 5 is all about retail credit accounts. A revolving credit account allows you to pay a minimum due per month and not the full outstanding balance. These accounts often report to Experian, sometimes also to D&B and Equifax. Due to how they report, these accounts help build business credit on a larger scale than Net 30 day vendors alone.

If you haven't completed Stage 1 through 4, there is no point in starting Stage 5. Why? Because you will most likely get a decline. These accounts check if your business credit foundation is set. They want to see if your business credit files are open. They may also check your bank rating, to see if you have some open vendor lines of credit. Often, they want to see your D&B file is open. In this stage it does not matter which retail credit card accounts you open and make purchases with. We have a great selection of companies offering products and services of value to any and all businesses.

Stage 6 - One Bank Loan, Why It Is Very Important and Exactly How to Get It

Stage 6 is all about getting more funding. Getting more credit makes your business more credible in the eyes of almost all other lenders. In Stage 6, we walk through what you must do to get funding to start the reporting process for your business. We show you how to place your business on all other lenders' radar.

What should you do if you are denied business credit?

As a creative, applying for loans is challenging. Denial can be a major blow to your progress as a professional artist. According to recent reports, as many as one third of applications for business loans get a denial. If you find yourself as part of that group, there are some ways to help the situation.

First, try to determine where the problem is. Possible areas of concern may include:

- Your business profits. Does your business have a healthy profit margin? Improving your profits by reducing and trimming operational excess and unnecessary business spending can help improve profits. This will boost your chances of approval.
- Your business assets and liabilities. If your balance sheet is out of whack, most lenders will run the other way. If your business is already heavy on debt, then this will be an area of concern you should address.

- Your payment histories and business credit profile. How you pay existing obligations will play a role in your approval or denial for credit. If you've gotten a business credit denial recently, check your business credit score and other payment performance data.

- Most payment information is only reported for 2 to 3 years (depending on the credit bureau), so if you've made a mistake or hit a bump or two in the road, don't let it worry you. Keep the positive payment history going, and make sure what is being reported is accurate.

- Your bank ratings. If your business bank account balances are often low, this can rule you out for certain types of business credit. Try to maintain $10,000 or more in your business bank accounts to avoid trouble.

The bottom line, if you've had a credit denial, then there is something about your business making it seem to be a bad risk. Your job is to analyze and understand your business credit report and business finances. Find where the problem is and take the necessary steps to correct your course. Sometimes a lack of history or data on your business is a key factor in a credit denial. You can fix this with careful steps to shape your business's financial picture and credit profile.

"Own nothing. Control Everything."

CHAPTER 7

FIND A WAY...

Creatives and entrepreneurs alike underestimate the power of business credit. A music and entertainment industry entrepreneur I know told me he knew about business credit, but wasn't using it. I was shocked! He had been conducting business for 15 years without access to business credit lines.

"Bro, you're crazy." I said.

After I broke things down for him, he had a big revelation. It was a "coming to Jesus" moment and he dug into business credit. With his entrepreneurial mindset, he got heavy into the details. After setting up those lines of business credit, he had access to enough capital to expand his business drastically. He used the funds to invest in a concert with popular rap artists from back in the day stacked on the lineup.

Most creatives think that because they have bad credit or no collateral, they have no chance to get loans. But there are actually many different financing options artists have. They can qualify even with severe credit challenges, even if they don't have collateral. As you already know, banks REQUIRE good credit AND collateral for business financing approval. But still, most people only go to their bank when they need money, because it's the only place they know to go to. But the most common business bank loans, SBA loans, only account for 1.1% of all business loans (Department of Revenue 2013). The reality is the big banks are NOT the suppliers of most business loans. And even though they require good credit and collateral to qualify, many sources don't.

The big banks are very conservative. Because of this, they often won't lend to creatives with challenged credit or there is no collateral. But artists can succeed even if they don't have perfect credit or don't have assets to pledge as collateral. Many business loans make good sense and have low enough risk based on other factors. This is so even if the owner doesn't have good credit and lacks collateral. So what types of funding can and can't you get with credit issues or if you lack collateral?

The 4 Cs of Business Lending

We've already covered the 5 Cs of Business Credit in Chapter 4. Now it's time to get into the 4 Cs of Business Lending. In lending when we look to see if a client is fundable, we are looking for one of these four Cs. But if you want money for your business, you only need one C to qualify.

The first C is **Cash Flow**. When you have an existing business with good cash flow you can qualify for business funding. Verifiable cash flow substantially increases your chances of funding approval. There are many funding programs you might qualify for including Business Revenue Lending.

If you don't have cash flow your business still might have **Collateral**, the second C. Collateral for your business is really your business assets. You can use many things as collateral. These include equipment, purchase orders, even account receivables. Having collateral greatly increases your chances of approval.

If you don't have cash flow or collateral, don't worry. You still can qualify for business funding. Lenders also look at your business credit to qualify you. **Business Credit** is our third C. Lenders may lend money based on your business credit profile and score. If you have a good business credit profile you can use that as security to get funding.

Maybe you are starting a new business, and you have no business credit, cash flow, or collateral. In this case, you can still qualify for funding. But lenders will use your personal credit to qualify you. **Personal Credit** is the fourth and final C that lenders will look at to approve you for funding. You can secure credit lines, through me, up to $250,000 with as low as a 650 credit score. These types of unsecured credit lines do not look at revenue or financials. Your credit is all they use to qualify you for funding.

All you need is one of the four Cs to qualify for much of the business financing available to you today.

Where NOT to go

Before you know where to get money if you have credit problems, you first should know where NOT to go. These sources might be appealing based on their offers and promotions. But they will not typically lend money if you have challenged personal credit. SBA loans, conventional bank financing, private investor money, and unsecured financing all have stringent credit requirements. SBA and other bank conventional loans are tough to qualify for. This is because the lender and SBA (Small Business Association) will check ALL aspects of the business and its owner for approval. To get approved, all aspects of the business and its owner's personal finances must be near PERFECT. There is no question SBA loans are tough to qualify for. This is why, per to the Small Business Lending Index, big banks deny over 89% of business applications.

Many people think when they have bad credit or lack collateral, a private investor is the best answer. But many investors will want an average or better credit score of 650 or higher. And they often want you to pledge some type of collateral. They might also want solid financials for at least two years. This means they want to see tax returns showing large net profits increasing over time. Think of private money as being for SBA and conventional bank loans that just miss the mark. Unsecured means no collateral is necessary for approval. No collateral GREATLY increases a lender's risk. No collateral requirements usually means it's the quality of credit determining qualification. You need good credit to qualify for any financing without collateral AND cash flow requirements.

Where TO go?

So where DO you go? There are many great funding options for creatives with personal credit issues or who lack collateral. They include revenue-based financing, asset-based financing, and equity financing. Also, they include crowdfunding and business credit. Or get unsecured financing using a credit partner/personal guarantor. The truth is, there is a LOT of capital out there that creative business owners can get. This is so even with personal credit issues or no collateral. Most of it isn't available through big banks. You can qualify for this massive amount of available financing based on your business strengths. This is as long as your business has even one strength. The big banks require your ENTIRE business and you to be near perfect to get money. But as you're about to discover, there are many other sources who will lend you money, even lots of it, based on just one strength. Long as you have a strength to offset your weakness of having bad credit or lacking collateral, you can get approval. These are often called compensating factors.

Cash-flow Based Financing

Many creative businesses have already proven concept and have consistent increasing sales. Their strength is they have shown stability and they can translate their talent into a growing business. The risk to the lender is less with established creative businesses. How are your sales? Sales are the difference between an untested concept or idea, and a viable business. Will your idea be well received? Do YOU know how to operate a business? Sales answer these questions.

If you have consistent sales, the next question is: does the business have existing cash flow proven by bank statements? There are lending options available only requiring a quick bank statement review. They won't even need to look at your tax returns. So even if your business shows a loss, you'll still be okay. The next question is: does the business have over $60,000 annually from credit card sales? Does the business have over $120,000 annually going through their bank account? If so, then revenue financing or a merchant advance might be the perfect funding product.

For this type of cash-flow-based financing, you must be in business six months. No startup businesses can qualify. You should have at least 10 monthly deposits going through your bank account, not just a few larger deposits. Most advertising you see for bad credit business financing are these products. These are short term advances of 6 – 18 months. They are mostly short term at first, such as 3 – 6-month terms. Then when half is paid down, the lender will lend more money at a longer term, such as 12 – 18 months. Loan amounts typically go up to $500,000. Your actual loan amount is based on your revenue. Usually, you can get a loan of 8 – 12% of annual revenue, based on verifiable revenue per your bank statements. For example, a company with $300,000 in sales might get a $30,000 advance to start. 500 credit scores are accepted for revenue and merchant financing. They are COMMON with this type of lending. Bad credit is okay, as long as you aren't actively in trouble such as in a bankruptcy. You cannot have serious recent and unresolved tax liens or judgments.

Depending on risk, cash flow financing rates of 10 – 45% are common. Risk factors include industry and time in business. More risk factors are bank statement details. These details include number of deposits, average daily balance, NSF charges, and amount of deposits monthly. Credit quality is another factor. Often rates are higher on first advance until you prove yourself to the lender. Tax returns, other income documents, and collateral are not required. You won't need to pledge any collateral to get approved. But you will typically be required to supply a personal guarantee. This is required for almost all business financing not accompanied by collateral.

Asset Based Financing

Asset based financing is also called collateral based lending. With this financing, the basis of your loan comes from the strength of your collateral. Since your collateral offsets the lender's risk, you can get approval with bad credit. You can still get REALLY good terms. Common BUSINESS collateral might include account receivables, inventory, and equipment. With account receivable financing you can secure up to 80% of receivables within 24 hours of approval. You must be in business for at least one year and receivables must be from another business. Rates are commonly 1.25 – 5%.

You can also use your inventory as collateral for financing and secure inventory financing. The smallest inventory loan amount is $150,000 and the general loan to value (cost) is 50%. Thus, inventory value would have to be $300,000 to qualify. Rates are normally 2% monthly on the outstanding loan balance. A typical borrower is a factory or retail store.

With equipment financing, lenders undervalue equipment by up to 50% and work with major equipment only. Lender won't combine a bunch of small equipment, and first and last month's payments are necessary to close. Loan amounts are available typically up to $2 million dollars. 401(k) and stocks are common PERSONAL collateral that can qualify for collateral-based lending. Use a 401(k) or IRAs to get up to 100% financing. Rates are usually less than 3%. A retirement plan is created, allowing for investment into the corporation. Funds roll over into the new plan. The new plan purchases stock in corporation and holds it. The corporation is debt-free and cash rich.

With securities-based lines of credit you can get an advance for up to 70 – 90% of the value of your stocks and bonds. These work much the same as 401(k) financing with similar terms and qualifications.

Equity Financing

With equity financing, you exchange a percentage of ownership in your business for financing, much like on the TV show Shark Tank. Personal credit is NOT an issue. You won't need to provide collateral. But equity investors are looking for a tested and proven concept. Sales help with approval. You might find some investors to invest in a concept only, or invention. But most will want to see you have an operating business earning money and making profits. And expect them to want a large piece of the equity. For it to be worth their time to invest, they might want 10 – 60% ownership of your business. That means they'll be taking a large part of your future earnings. It's something you want to consider before recruiting an investor.

Business Credit and Unsecured Credit

Business credit is a great way to get money because approvals are not based on personal credit. No collateral is necessary for approval. Business credit reports usually start with a few vendor accounts offering initial credit. Initial accounts create tradelines and a credit profile which establish a score. The company's new profile and score are used to get credit. Newly-obtained credit is based on the company's credit per the EIN, not the owner's credit based on the SSN. Personal credit doesn't matter as the credit linked to the EIN is used for approval.

When you use vendors to build initial credit, they may want your SSN on the application for identification purposes. But you can still apply for business credit based solely on your EIN at most retail stores. You can get cash credit also, like high-limit cards with MasterCard. But building business credit all starts with vendor accounts. Without them, you won't be able to start your credit profile. Building a profile is the key to getting cash and retail credit cards for your business.

Once you apply for vendor credit, use your credit. It takes about 1 – 3 months for those accounts to report to the business credit bureaus. Make sure the vendor you are using reports to the business credit bureaus, because not all of them do. Once those accounts are reported, a business has a business credit profile and score. This can be used to get retail credit cards next. Once you have about more payment experiences reporting, you can start to get cash credit like MasterCard accounts. A payment experience is the reporting of an account to one business credit bureau.

Unsecured credit requires no collateral, but it DOES require good credit. But if you have credit issues, you can still get approval if you have a good credit partner. Or you can work with someone who will sign as a guarantor, who has good credit. The guarantor is then liable for the business debt in case the account defaults. Approval amounts range from $10,000 to $150,000. Card limits are equal to what the signer has on their credit now. These accounts often report to the business credit bureaus. So, they also help build your business credit. And they are NOT reported on the guarantor's personal credit report. Your guarantor will need excellent personal credit to qualify.

Obtain Money Based on Your Business Strengths

When you apply at a conventional lender they want to review everything. They look at your business P&L statement, balance sheet, tax returns, business and personal financials, business and personal credit, revenue, collateral, and so on. It's hard to believe anyone gets approved considering how much information is under scrutiny. What most business owners don't know is you can get money for your business based on company strengths. This is without all these items coming under review.

Every business has its strengths and weaknesses. When a lender requires such extensive documentation, often they find the company's weakness. Once they find the weakness they then use it as an excuse to deny the application. And they will not lend the business owner the much-needed funding. But when a lender only looks at a company's strengths, then there is the best chance of getting approval for the most amount of money. Some businesses have collateral as their strengths. These include purchase orders, account receivables, and credit card sales. They also include equipment, inventory, and commercial real estate. And they include cash flow, or other business assets. Some business owners have 401(k)s, IRAs, or other securities they can use as their strength to secure funding.

Be creative when it comes to collateral. Your brand may have more strengths than you think. It's always easiest to get financing when you know what you are looking for. Now you know some of the many financing options available to creatives.

Let's Review

Lucky for creative entrepreneurs, there are A LOT of different viable financing options. This is even if you have challenged personal credit or lack collateral. The key is to know where NOT to look, and not waste your time. And know where TO look, the places which will approve you based on your strengths.

With personal or business collateral, you might qualify for financing right now. If you have a cash flow of more than $10,000 monthly, you might qualify for cash-flow-based financing right now. With a partner or other party to sign as a guarantor, unsecured financing is another good funding option. Business credit is still an easy and fast way to get your hands on money. This is even if you have no collateral, no cash flow, no guarantor, and bad credit.

"The right mindset will open up your whole financial universe."

CHAPTER 8

WHAT'S THE SCORE?

One of the most confusing parts of understanding the wonderful world of credit is the breakdown of credit scores. Navigating the analytical side with numbers and statistics is often a challenge for the free-spirited creative mind. In this chapter, we will cover everything you need to know to understand your credit score and how it affects your creative business.

FICO Scores Decoded

Let's discover just how easily and quickly you can obtain excellent FICO Credit Scores regardless of your personal credit quality right now.

FICO's History

FICO is a business analytic software company. Their base is in San Jose, California. FICO was founded by Bill Fair and Earl Isaac in 1956. Their FICO score has become the main credit score used to determine consumer credit risk. FICO started off as Fair, Isaac and Company. William Fair, one of the original founders, was an engineer by trade. Earl Isaac, the other founder, was a mathematician by trade. The two met while working at the Stanford Research Institute in Menlo Park California. In 1958, FICO pitched its first credit risk analysis system to 50 American lenders.

FICO went public in 1986 and is traded on the New York Stock Exchange under the ticker symbol FICO. The company debuted its first general-purpose FICO score in 1989. Scores come from credit reports and range from 300 to 850. Lenders use the scores to gauge a potential borrower's creditworthiness. Fair, Isaac and Company's name became Fair Isaac Corporation in 2003. The company rebranded again in 2009. It is now FICO, making their name the same as the signature FICO score they offer. First, their base was in San Rafael, California. They moved to Minneapolis in 2004. They then moved back to San Jose, California in 2013.

FICO Scores: What You Should Know

The most widely used credit score is the FICO Score. This score is a mathematical model. It depicts a consumer's risk of going 90 days late on an account within the next 24 months. Lenders use the FICO Score to help them make billions of credit decisions every year. The FICO Score comes from information in consumer credit reports kept at credit reporting agencies. FICO credit scores range from 300 to 850.

A FICO Score is a mathematical equation checking many types of information from your credit report. A FICO Score estimates your level of future credit risk. This is by comparing this information to patterns in hundreds of thousands of past credit reports. You have three FICO credit scores. There is one for each of the three credit bureaus: Equifax, TransUnion, and Experian. Each FICO Score comes from information the credit bureau keeps on file about you. The FICO Score from each credit reporting agency considers only the data in your credit reports at that agency. Your credit score may be different at each of the main credit reporting agencies. If your current scores from the credit reporting agencies differ, it's probably because the data those agencies have on you differs. If your information is identical at all three credit reporting agencies, each FICO Score should be very close.

To calculate a FICO Score, your credit report must contain enough information. And it must be recent enough. Often that means you must have at least one account open for six months or longer. Plus you need at least one account on a report to the credit reporting agency within the last six months.

Finally!!! The Answer to Why You Have So Many Credit Scores

There are MANY different credit scores out there. There are credit scores consumers can pull themselves through credit monitoring. And there are mortgage scores, auto scores, and many more. There are actually over 16 different credit scorecards existing today with FICO alone. Each of these scorecards reflects different credit scores. These scorecards help particular industries better gauge credit risk. The mortgage industry, for example, cares more about a consumer's past mortgage history than anything else. So they weigh home loan history heavier into the total score calculation than other accounts. A consumer's credit monitoring score might be 660. But then when they apply for a mortgage their score might be much lower. This can be due to some past negative mortgage accounts on the report. Their mortgage score might even be higher than their consumer score if they have past positive mortgage accounts. A credit score which a consumer pulls themselves will not be the same as their Mortgage Industry Option Score. This is the scores lenders and brokers use to access mortgage default risk. Their mortgage score won't be the same as their auto score that car dealers pull, either.

These different credit scorecards help specific industries better determine risk. With so many industries that offer credit, there are just as many credit scores available. Plus, different scores come from different companies, creating even more credit scores. FICO is the biggest provider of consumer credit scores. Now even the credit bureaus are in the credit scoring game with their Vantage score.

The Credit Bureaus' Secret Credit Score

Vantage Score is the credit bureaus' own credit score, meant to compete with FICO. The three bureaus unveiled the Vantage Score on March 14, 2006. All three main credit reporting agencies use the same formula to calculate it. Vantage Score has scores as high as 990 while FICO scores can only be as high as 850. A 700 FICO score reflects good consumer credit. But a 700 Vantage score reflects below-average personal credit.

Here are Vantage Score 2.0 risk levels. "A" credit scores range from 900 – 990. "B" credit scores range from 800 – 899. "C" credit scores range from 700 – 799. "D" credit scores range from 600 – 699, and "F" credit scores range from 501 – 599. Scores going up to 990 versus FICO scores going up to 850 have created an issue with lenders. This is one of the main reasons that Vantage Score hasn't become widely accepted. So the bureaus have now changed their score range with Vantage Score 3.0, from 2013. The new Vantage Score only goes to 850, mimicking the FICO top score.

How Credit Scores Are Calculated - The Inside Scoop

Fair Isaac and Vantage Score hold their credit scoring formulas as a close secret. This is much like the formula for Coca-Cola or your grandma's legendary double chocolate chip cookies. This can be very frustrating for consumers when they see remarks on the credit report like "too many revolving debt accounts." They may not know exactly what that means. Fair Isaac and Vantage Score have issued some public information about how they calculate credit scores.

Payment History

The top-rated factor for both models is payment history. This is because lenders want to know a person's payment history – past and present. This category can break down into three subcategories:

- Recency: This is the last time a payment was late. The more time that passes the better.
- Frequency: One late payment looks a heck of a lot better than a dozen
- Severity: A payment 30 days late is not as serious as a payment 60 or 120 days late.

Collections, tax liens, foreclosures, repossessions, charge-offs, and bankruptcies are credit score killers.

Improving Your Scores

You can improve this aspect of your score by paying your bills on time. Make sure you have a lot of accounts you are paying as agreed to offset the accounts not paid as agreed.

How Much is Owed

The score looks at the total amount owed on all accounts as well as how much you owe on different types of accounts (mortgage, auto, etc.). Using a higher percentage of the credit limits will worry lenders and hurt the credit score. People who max out their limits have a much greater risk of default.

Utilization

For revolving debit-credit cards, the formula looks at the difference between the high limit and balances. For example, let's say your customer has a MasterCard with a credit limit of $10,000 and they have spent $2,000 of it. This is a 20% utilization ratio. The lower the ratio, the higher the credit score. So, if you are looking for a quick credit score boost, pay down any accounts you can.

With FICO, 30% of your credit score comes from utilization, while 35% comes from payment history. Utilization is the second-highest weighted aspect of your scores. If you are overusing revolving accounts, you can damage your scores as much as if you were paying late each month. Using anything over 30% of your limit will lower your credit scores. Adding high-limit credit cards to your report can also SIGNIFICANTLY and quickly raise your scores. This is sometimes by as much as 100 points or more.

One more important tidbit, CLOSED ACCOUNTS do not help and can hurt if there is a balance remaining. A long-perpetuated myth has been to close accounts not in use. But this hurts consumers in several ways. As you now know, overall and individual account utilization plays a major role in credit scoring. If consumers close old accounts, the overall utilization rate will increase. This will cause the score to decrease.

Length of Credit History and Depth of Credit

This is less important than the previous factors, but it still matters. It considers (1) the age of the oldest account and (2) the average age of all your accounts. It is possible to have a good score with a short history. But often the longer, the better. Many people can still have high credit scores if the other factors are positive. With FICO, this is the third-largest aspect of the score calculation.

If a person is new to credit then there is little they can do to improve a credit score. You cannot backdate any newly-added accounts to improve this score aspect. You can get added as an authorized user to a family member's account that has been in long-standing. That can improve this aspect of your score.

The average age of accounts is another important reason to keep all accounts open. If a consumer has had many accounts for some time but don't use them, they still benefit. This is from the average age of the accounts open in their credit file. Also make sure you use each of your accounts at least once every six months. Credit issuers must reserve the money they offer in credit limits for their clients' use. So they don't like having accounts sitting dormant that are not making them money. If an account sits dormant for a long enough time, many creditors cancel it due to inactivity. CRAs will claim an account is inactive if there has been no activity in the most recent six month period. An inactive account does not benefit your score as much as an active account.

New Credit / Recent Credit

New credit is not always a bad thing. But opening new accounts can hurt a credit score. This can happen if a consumer applies for lots of credit in a short time and doesn't have a long credit history. The score factors in how many accounts the consumer applied for recently, how many new accounts the consumer has opened, how much time since the consumer's credit application, and how much time since the consumer opened an account. The model looks for rate shopping. Shopping for a mortgage or an auto loan may cause many lenders to request your credit report many times each. This is even though a person is only looking for one loan. Auto dealers are notorious for running 3 – 15 credit reports. This is called shotgunning the credit. To compensate for this, the score counts many auto and mortgage-specific inquiries in any 30 day period as one inquiry. The specific calculation for cutoff dates and types is confusing.

For most people, a credit inquiry won't have an impact on their credit score. Groupings of inquiries WILL adversely affect scores. But inquiries have a greater impact if you have few accounts or a short credit history. Many inquiries also mean greater risk. People with six inquiries or more on their credit reports are eight times more likely to declare bankruptcy than those with no inquiries. This is per MyFico.com.

FICO 9: What You Should Know

FICO's newest credit score is the FICO 9. This new score includes many changes from prior FICO models. Medical collections no longer score the same as regular collections. Now they count much less. A consumer with a 711 credit score, whose only negative collection issue is medical-related, will see a 25 point score increase. Other changes to the model will better gauge if a consumer with limited credit history can repay a prospective debt. The business calls this a thin file. These people might not have a score in the past. But they will now with the new version.

Non-traditional credit, such as your residential rental history, will be under consideration. This means consumers with little to no credit history but pay rent on time will get a boost. FICO 9 ignores paid-off and settled collections. Under the old FICO model, if you let an account go into collection, your credit score took a hit for as long as that collection is on the credit report. This was seven years. Now, the score ignores any collection with a zero balance. This is HUGE. Paying off collections used to prolong how long the account stayed on your reports. It could result in more damage.

5 Quick Tips to Raise Your FICO Score

1. Pay your bills on time and beg for forgiveness if you pay late.
2. Have lots of positive credit on your report. And make sure you use it at least every six months. Don't forget a good credit mix.

3. Keep open credit cards; three is best. Keep balances low. Get the highest credit limit accounts you can get.

4. If your credit file is new, get added as an authorized user but only on a FAMILY MEMBER's account.

5. Do NOT apply for too much credit all at once unless buying a car or home. Then do your shopping within 30 days.

The Dun and Bradstreet PAYDEX Business Credit Score

The main credit score used in the business world is the PAYDEX score from Dun and Bradstreet. This number assesses a business's lending risk. It is much the same as a consumer credit score reflects a consumer's individual credit risk.

PAYDEX is more or less the business equivalent of your personal credit score. The exact definition from Dun & Bradstreet is: The D&B PAYDEX® Score is D&B's unique dollar-weighted numerical indicator of how a firm paid its bills over the past year, based on trade experiences reported to D&B by various vendors.

There are many BIG differences between a business PAYDEX credit score and an individual FICO consumer credit score. Consumer FICO credit scores range from 350 – 850. The PAYDEX Score ranges from 0 – 100. 100 is the highest score you can get. Individual credit scores come from several factors. The PAYDEX score comes from one single factor. It's if a business makes prompt payments to its suppliers and creditors within the agreed-upon terms of payment.

Most lenders and suppliers are looking for a score of 70 and higher. A score of 80 or better is very good. If you own a business, your PAYDEX score is essential in establishing new credit and continuing to build credit limits exceeding $100,000. It only takes 60 days to establish a positive PAYDEX credit score. First, apply for a DUNS Number. This is a nine-digit business identifying number with Dun and Bradstreet.

Once your DUNS number is established you should next find a merchant who will extend you credit and then report that credit to Dun and Bradstreet. Once you have a positive business credit report to Dun and Bradstreet you will have a positive PAYDEX score established. Then apply for more business credit and use it often. Make sure you pay back early to raise your scores to 80 or higher.

You can easily and quickly establish a positive PAYDEX credit score. As you continue to pay your bills on time, your scores will continue to rise. This makes it possible to qualify for credit in your business name.

Experian's Business Credit Scores

The second most popular credit score in the business world is the Experian Intelliscore. Experian's most recent score system is Intelliscore Plus. They boast of it as the next level in credit scoring. Intelliscore Plus takes into account hundreds of variables to offer a business score between 0 – 100. Intelliscore predicts a business's risk of going seriously delinquent, or over 91 days late. Or having a major financial issue like bankruptcy in the next 12 months. The new Intelliscore Plus has over 800 aggregates or factors affecting the score. Experian looks at business data segments like firmographics, public records, collections, and trade information. It then places each business in one of three different models. Intelliscore is one of the only business scores offering a blended score.

The Blended/ Owner Model, blends commercial data and the owner's consumer information. Because this score blends with consumer data, it is one of the only scores where someone needs your permission to pull. A study showed that when trouble hit a business, blended scores dropped an average of 30% over the four quarters leading up to the bad event. Their consumer scores of the owner showed no statistically significant decline over the same period. The score evaluates personal information on the owner as it relates to business performance. Experian says their research data shows 53% of business problems first showed up as credit problems on business credit reports. 46% of problems first showed up on the owner's personal report. Blended scores outperform consumer or business alone by 10 – 20%. Intelliscore Plus, like FICO, has multiple facets to the entire score makeup. There are five different components comprising the Intelliscore.

Experian's Intelliscore Breakdown:

- Historical Behavior 5 – 10%
- Age, Industry, Size 5 – 10%
- Credit Utilization 10 – 15%
- Derogatory items 10 – 15%
- Payments, Balances 50 – 60%

Scores are based on many factors in your business credit report. These are: Number of trade experiences, Outstanding balances, Payment habits, Credit utilization, and Trends over time. And they also include Public record recency, frequency and dollar amount and demographics like years on file. Further, they include Standard Industrial Classification codes and business size. The Intelliscore is "calculated by a statistically derived algorithm, designed to determine risk based on multiple factors."

- Credit: Number of trade experiences, balances outstanding, payment habits, credit utilization and trends over time.
- Public Records: Recency, frequency and dollar amounts associated with liens, judgments or bankruptcies.
- Demographic Information: Years on file, Standard Industrial Classification (SIC) code and business size.

Experian also offers a Financial Stability Risk Score. This score predicts the potential of a business going bankrupt or defaulting on its obligations. FSR scores range from 1 – 100 and they break down into five Risk Classes with Class 1 being the lower risk. Equifax's Business Credit Scores Equifax's main business credit scoring model is the Credit Risk Score. Equifax created this score to predict the probability of a business customer becoming seriously delinquent. A lower score indicates a higher risk of serious delinquency (90 days late) in a 12 month period. Credit scores range from 1 – 100.

Like the D&B PAYDEX score, the Credit Risk Score comes from payment history. All that's necessary for a good score is to pay business obligations as agreed. The earlier payments are made, the higher the score is.

Equifax's Credit Risk Score:

- Paid as Agreed 90 +
- 1 – 30 days overdue 80 89
- 31 – 60 days overdue 60 – 79
- 61 – 90 days overdue 40 – 59
- 91 – 120 days overdue 20 – 39
- 120+ overdue 1 – 19

Equifax also provides a business credit score for suppliers, the Small Business Credit Risk Score for Suppliers. This model is designed to help credit grantors improve their risk assessment. And it is to reduce delinquency rates while helping improve profitability. The score uses unique bank loans, lease information, credit card data, and supplier, Telco and utility credit history. It also uses public records and firmographic data from their own Equifax Commercial database. These scores range from 101 – 816. Experian offers several other popular scores used by suppliers, lenders, vendors, and credit issuers.

The Credit Risk Score predicts the likelihood of a business incurring a 90 days severe delinquency or charge-off over the next 12 months. The Business Failure Score predicts the likelihood of a business failure through formal or informal bankruptcy over the next 12 months. The Payment Index provides a dollar weighted index of a business's current and past payment performance. It is based on all payment experiences in the Equifax Commercial database. Equifax also offers a Business Failure Risk Score with many reports. This score predicts the likelihood the business will fail or file for bankruptcy in the next 12 months. This model helps identify businesses that pose a greater risk for failure. This way, suppliers and credit grantors can take appropriate actions.

The FICO SBSS Score

The FICO SBSS score is a measure of your small business's creditworthiness. This score is becoming very popular with lenders. This score has also become widely used by SBA to qualify business loans. It comes from both personal and business credit history. The SBSS was launched in 1993 when the SBA started using it to evaluate all 7 (a) loans under $350,000. In 2014, it became even more popular. Scores reflect the likelihood of the applicant paying their bills timely. SBSS scores range from 0 – 300. Higher scores are better and mean lower risk. Personal and business credit history, plus financial data figure into the total score. As of 2014, all SBA 7(a) loans must go through a business credit score prescreen. For SBA loans, you won't get approval with a score below 140. But they often set the cutoff as high as 160. Below that, you'll probably get a denial because of being too high a risk. And chances are good the SBA lender won't even submit your application to the SBA if your score does not meet this threshold. Many factors are taken into account to calculate the FICO SBSS score. Some include the owner or co-owner's personal credit information. They can include business credit history, age of business, years in business, and financial data like assets. Other score factors include cash flow, revenue, the last 12 months of PAYDEX scores from D&B, liens, judgments and any other known financial data. If you have no business credit history and limited time in business, the highest possible FICO SBSS score you can get is 140. But to get a score as high as that, you must have pristine personal credit if no business credit is established.

SBSS models are validated for term loans, lines of credit, and commercial cards all the way up to $1 million. This helps credit issuers make evaluations for larger transactions. If you are applying for bank financing of $1 million or less, chances are good your SBSS score is being evaluated. SBSS gives small business credit issuers different combinations of data to check the risk of a business. For example, a credit issuer can choose to only consider the application data of the principle owner. Or they can choose to also include data from one or more business bureaus. Or they can choose to weight one aspect higher than another. This is a highly intelligent score. It automatically goes from one business bureau to another in whatever order or priority the credit issuer chooses, to generate a score. So if a lender prefers the D&B PAYDEX score as the default, the SBSS pulls that data set. If there isn't enough info to generate a score, it automatically checks another business score like the Experian Intelliscore. Or it can even move onto Equifax commercial data.

"A good business credit profile and score can be the difference between having a prosperous creative career or being at the helm of a sinking ship."

CHAPTER 9

PRIVATE INVESTORS

Another tool in the tool kit of creative funding is using private investors. A private investor is anyone with disposable income above their own needs. A part of their financial portfolio probably already deals with investments, so they are looking for opportunities to diversify their income streams. This person is willing to invest with the hope of a return on their investment. They are usually a risk-taker, open to hearing a proposal. While most private investors are going to be unfamiliar with investing in entertainment or backing a creative project, these types of investors do exist, and others will still be intrigued by new ways of making money.

Many investors in creative industries have a creative spark, drive, or interest themselves, but have never had the opportunity to fully pursue it. They might already be somehow involved in entertainment and familiar with what you are doing. Somehow, they connect with a potential creator and are attracted to their ideas and projects. It could really be anyone, though. The ideal private investor is anyone interested in investing in you. This could be a friend, family member, boss, neighbor, coworker, etc. They could be anywhere!

There are good places to start looking for one, though. The key to finding them is through networking. Get out in your local community and start talking about what you do. Join associations and organizations like investment clubs to meet people already on the hunt for opportunities. You can also attend small business seminars and workshops. Go to where the money is. People attending these types of events are specifically there for business opportunities. When you talk to a potential investor, let them know what it is you are doing and what you bring to the table. Networking is key to finding a private investor. Remember, "Your network determines your net worth!"

One tip for approaching a private investor is to use a "soft sell." Casually ask their opinion on whatever it is you are working on. Say something like, "Hey, can I send you a song? I'd love to hear what you think."

People love to share their opinion. They want to feel like their perspective matters. It makes them feel valued. Then, if they give you positive feedback, ask them if this is something they would be interested in investing in, or do they know someone who might be interested in investing. There's no exact science to it. Just put yourself in a position to ask. The worst they'll say is no, but then you will know. Don't be afraid to put yourself out there. It's a vulnerable space, but you'll need to be comfortable with being uncomfortable to grow.

It's tough asking for money, and even harder to ask for the large amounts you actually need for certain creative projects. It's one thing to ask for $20, but to ask someone for $200,000—that's a whole different kind of ask. Can we shift that frame of thought? Consider that money is relative. It might not be such a far-fetched request if you are approaching someone with billions at their disposal. You never know until you ask. This could be just a drop in the bucket for them.

As long as you are pitching to the right investor, money usually isn't the problem with accepting a proposal; it's a problem with understanding. Most investors you talk to will have little to no experience investing in a creator or an artistic project. This is a different type of transaction that will be new and intimidating for them at first. If you don't know how to explain the details of the potential return on their investment and answer questions, then they will reject your offer. You need a translator, someone who can speak the language. You may be talented with your art, but if you can't speak the business lingo and lack investment vocabulary, you either need to learn as much as you can on the subject to make a compelling pitch OR, you need to get someone on your team who can.

Here's a tip! Consider having a professional there to explain the financial benefits of investing in your work. I recently worked with a female rapper with a pilot friend who had profited greatly after investing in the stock market. At first, when she approached the pilot about investing in her career, he was uninterested. Later, she asked him again, but this time, she brought me on as an advisor to share my insight on both the music industry and investing.

"I'm going to be honest with you," he said when we got to talking. "I invest in stocks. Bitcoin. Foreign exchange. This is not my wheelhouse."

Since I was familiar with how investing in an artist like this works, I was able to break down the financial opportunity being offered to him. I negotiated the details, using proper terminology which ultimately made the deal more appealing since he could now see this as a viable investment. This pilot finally moved forward and ended up investing $100,000 into the female rapper. Having someone who knows what they are talking about is essential to making deals with private investors. There are people out there with the wherewithal to invest in your project, it's all about finding them, and presenting them with the opportunity. Again, this is all relative. A mountain for you could be a molehill for them.

The majority of private investors have no experience with this type of investing. There are lots of types of investors. There are investors who invest in stocks, Bitcoin, and real estate. Many of them just don't understand how you can make money off of a movie, or a song, or a book. This is why it is so important to have someone who can translate this concept in a way they can understand. The risk is much different when you are investing in a creative venture. You aren't investing in a company or property; you are investing in a person. A lot can happen to a person over time. What happens to the investment if you fall ill and fail to complete the project? What happens if you end up in legal trouble? What happens if you just quit? These are all risks involved with this type of investing.

An investor friend of mine struggled with his early investments in creatives. He started off by investing in a few Spanish music groups out of the Bronx. One group didn't want to listen to professional advice and failed to reach an audience, while the other group just stopped making music together.

He ended up losing $100,000 twice! By his third attempt, he was unwilling to invest such a large amount because of the risk involved.

Because there is so much risk involved in this type of investing, it is absolutely crucial to lawyer up. Depending on the dollar amount, you might have to have a lawyer anyways. You'll want to be as careful as possible with the legal paperwork and registration protocol for your state. Recognize that because of the risk involved, there is legal language in the contracts that might sound really bad. There are disclaimers and disclosures of all the possible outcomes involved with this agreement. This is a sobering moment for many investors, and signing the contracts is when it gets real. They have to really believe in you to take on that risk. This is why is important to demonstrate the value you have to offer and the viability of what you are offering. It helps to have already monetized your creative work in some way to prove the viability of the investment.

You'll have a difficult time asking a bank for money to become an actor, rapper, or musician. They don't care about your art. They don't even care about you as a person. Even a solid business plan doesn't matter much to a bank. They are trained to only look at the numbers involved with your credit history. The chances of a creative securing a loan through traditional lending methods are slim to none. With private investors, however, it becomes a much more personal experience. Securing one means you've transferred the dream to another person. They can see your vision and believe in it. By investing in your art, they become connected to you, and what you are trying to do. Your private investor is essentially one of your biggest fans because they are financially linked to your success.

There are a whole variety of investors out there. They might be hands-off, and leave all the creative work to you, or they might be more hands-on, with advice to offer you on your creative journey. Some people invest in concerts, some invest in festivals or entire tours. There are investors for movies, books, and just a single show. The world of investing is vast, sophisticated, and complex. Again, this is why it is so important to have someone involved in these negotiations who understands how it all works. Someone who understands the talent side, financial side, and legal side becomes an important commodity on your team.

There are investors who invest in concerts. Invest in festivals. Invest in movies. There might be multiple investors involved in a single show. Or a tour. Or a movie. A one-off. All different types of investors and all different types of situations. It is vast, complex, sophisticated. It's a small elite class of people who are willing to do it. Someone like Rob becomes an important commodity because he understands all of that. You have to know enough about an industry and the financial aspect to put it together and present it to an investor. Investor side. Talent side. Legal side. All must come together for the transfer of that money.

Don't make the mistake of only looking at private investors as financial people. They could be anyone. They could be family, friends, or colleagues. Remain open to the idea that investors can come in many different shapes and forms. Everyone is a potential investor and any amount is an investment. Take an example of a mother with a daughter who wants to be a singer. If she pulls money out of her 401K to help get her daughter's career started, that mother is now an investor. The world of private investors is broad. Cast the net wide and you might catch a marlin!

"Your network determines your net worth."

CHAPTER 10

THE FRIENDS AND FAMILY PLAN

Although business credit is our preferred way of gaining funds for your creative business, it isn't a get-rich-quick method. It takes time, sometimes years, to build those lines. For some artists, they need money now. If you don't have good personal credit or large sums saved up, getting a creative project off the ground can be a daunting task. The easiest way for some artists to get support is often by asking for help from those who know them best. There is comfortability in taking the path of least resistance. Talking to friends and family is familiar and less stressful than approaching a bank or traditional lender. It's a lot easier to ask mom and dad for cash than it is a stranger in a business suit. Often, your friends and family already know about your passion. They already support you and want to see you succeed. Compared to using credit or finding a private investor, this is low-hanging fruit. That's also why the Friends and Family Plan is the go-to method for creatives who are just starting out.

One thing to know about the Friends and Family Plan, is that it can be a double-edged sword. While some are very comfortable asking their buddies and relatives for money, there are those who find this deeply uncomfortable. People get real funny when it comes to money. With pride and ego all wrapped up in someone's financial status, they act strange when you ask for a loan. Depending on the situation, asking might even jeopardize the relationship. Not to mention, if you've asked before and received nothing, you might be afraid of more rejection. Some creatives really struggle to ask for help. And not everyone has a good relationship with their family. Their response could depend on your history and reputation. Often, talent doesn't even matter when it is overshadowed by circumstance. People may be hesitant to help if you have a track record of losing jobs, getting in trouble with the law, or repeatedly checking in and out of rehab. These can all be stacked against you. Sometimes it's not necessarily that they doubt you, instead, they doubt the entire industry. What you are attempting may be so far outside of their comfort zone, that they don't believe it can be done.

Asking friends and family can work for you or against you, depending on the details of the situation. On one side, you have Sammie. Sammie does well in school. Sammie always wins. Of course, everyone is going to support Sammie. On the reverse side, Sammie was always in trouble. In and out of jail. Rehab. Everyone in the neighborhood loves Sammie and thinks he's dope, but when he comes to them asking for money, they are hesitant. It's frustrating for a creative in this situation. This can be a complicated situation. If they've had a hard time just getting by, this opportunity might help them turn their life around. Maybe the whole reason why they struggled is that they never saw their art as a legitimate plan in the first place. They couldn't make their dreams a reality and just didn't know what else to do. They can't make it in the traditional workforce because they've been on the wrong path all along. For a creative, this can be devastating.

Approaching friends and family doesn't have to be scary. Instead, make it fun! Plan an event. Invite them over for dinner. Friends and family already get together for all sorts of reasons, like watching sports games, playing cards, and a whole laundry list of life event celebrations. Avoid making it too formal or it might get weird. Just keep it light and casual. As you invite your guests, explain to them you want to talk to them about something you've been working on. By making the gathering enjoyable and purposeful, people will be more likely to support you. You'll probably get a good turnout from those who care about you the most. Who better to pitch your ideas to than those who already want you to succeed?

When addressing your tribe for financial support, have a game plan. Plan out your budget and figure out exactly what you need before you ask. Write down exactly what you are going to tell them. The act of writing something out is very powerful. Statistics say you are 40% more likely to achieve your goals if you write them down. It helps you get clear on what you want to accomplish and will motivate you to stick to them. Prepare a small presentation. Maybe you create a PowerPoint or print out a One Sheet. Share some of your work with them too. Maybe you play some of your music, display some of your art, or screen one of your films. Show them what you are doing and explain how they can help you do even more. Make them see your vision and understand your creative mission.

Even if only a few people show up and even fewer actually jump on the opportunity to invest in your request, remind yourself that these are the ones in your circle who truly believe you have something of value. No amount of support is too small. You might be surprised at who will chip in and how much you can raise. Presenting your ideas to others will also give you great confidence. Approaching friends and family first can also be great practice for talking about your art in the future. At the end of the event, you'll be closer to your dream than you were when you started.

Because these are informal relationships, most people won't view this as an investment. Occasionally you might have an uncle who has a background in business, a friend who is a lawyer, or a relative who is just a stickler for protocol. In these instances, you can sign documents, like a notarized promissory note, and make it a more legitimate investment opportunity. Quite often, though, no contracts are drawn up and this will be more of a verbal agreement. These people are often acting out of the goodness of their heart, happy to help a friend or relative. This is a jaded viewpoint which often makes the transaction very casual. Unless you are already established with your creative business, they won't see it as an investment. They might view this simply as a novelty.

The Do's and Don'ts of The Friends and Family Plan

- DO your research! Do your homework before you approach friends and family. Get some data together. Give examples of others who have done it before. Make real-life examples part of your presentation.

- DO plan an event. Rather than approaching one person at a time, organize a gathering. Rent a space, host them at your house, offer them dinner. You could even get it catered! Lots of people will turn up for free food! Plus, events create a buzz and raise the level of importance.

- DO practice and prepare. Put your best foot forward with a polished, well-thought-out, organized presentation. Regardless of relationships, you still need to provide a viable business opportunity when you ask anyone to invest in you.

- DO have a mechanism of presentation. It could be a pdf of your creative portfolio. It could be an EPK, a video, or a song. People are very visual.

- DO share your work. Show off your talent. Let your potential investors see what they will be supporting. Offer them a sample.

- DO prepare a budget in advance. Figure out exactly how much money you need, what you need it for, and how you will use it. Avoid having to come back asking for more after the initial investment. If you find that you need more money later, it can be a red flag to an investor, suggesting that you don't know what you are doing financially. Breaking it down in an organized document will be appreciated by the analytically minded friends and family members. Also, make note of the potential returns they can expect on their investment.

- DON'T over ask. Never ask for more than you need. Exaggerating and overborrowing on your loans will put you in unnecessary debt and strain the relationship.

- DON'T ignore your debts for too long. Pay everyone back in a timely manner and have a plan for how you will do this.

- DO pay people back. Consider the worst-case scenario and what you will do if things don't work out. If you value these people and these relationships, then you need an exit strategy and plan B.

Consider the risks involved with what you are doing. Make a plan for paying others back so you don't damage any relationships.

- DON'T be a pest. Don't overdo it and hassle people too much. It's okay to follow up with anyone who wants more time to think about it, but be careful not to come on too strong. People will start avoiding you if this becomes annoying.

- DON'T borrow money from someone you have a romantic relationship with. A marriage is a little different because it is a legally binding situation and you are financially tied to each other as a team. With any other type of intimate relationship, however, emotions get involved. Avoid any business interactions with these people. The Business of Love is a dangerous game to play.

- DO suggest having something in writing. This can be as informal as an email or as formal as a contract drawn up by an attorney. Determine this based on your needs and the preferences of the investor. If they don't want to use a contract, that's fine, but offering it demonstrates how serious you are about this opportunity. Just offer it and let them reject it if they choose to. I recommend using a promissory note. It's a simple document where a person promises to pay another back. You can get it from a place like Staples and have it notarized at the bank. It's totally legit and legally binding.

- DO involve a lawyer for large sums of money. I strongly recommend talking to an attorney, especially when the amount involved in an investment is substantial.

- DO meet with a money-minded professional. Often the business side is not the strength of creatives. We strongly recommend creatives meet with a financial advisor, accountant, or someone who can help create the appropriate documents for your budget. If you need help, they can paint the financial picture for investors by explaining how funds will be utilized and when they can expect a return on their investment. The more professional, organized, and official it is, the better.

- DO keep your investment funds separate from your personal finances. Use a separate bank account. Don't let the loan for your creative project get mixed up with your bill money unless living expenses are a part of your budget.

- DO consider all expenses, including your basic survival needs. This is particularly important if you plan to quit your day job or shift to part-time. If you plan to reduce the number of hours you work at the job currently supporting you to work on your creative project, disclose this information with friends and family. Factor in your living expense under an altered work situation and how long it will take to monetize your brand to a level where it is supporting you.

The Bible says, "Ask and it will be given to you; seek and you will find; knock and the door will be opened to you." (Matthew 7:7).

People underestimate the capacity for compassion others have for us. You never know until you ask, so just ask. It sounds simple, but we know this can be difficult to do. We often hold ourselves back psychologically. We mentally build up our pride and struggle to ask for help when it comes to money. Whatever it is holding you back, figure out how to overcome it. If you struggle speaking to family and friends about your dreams now, how will you fare in the future when you are negotiating with a private investor, publisher, booking agent, record label, production company, or entertainment industry executive? Don't let your ego get in the way of your own success. Just ask. Remember, "closed mouths don't get fed."

"Ask and it will be given to you; seek and you will find; knock and the door will be opened to you." (Matthew 7:7)

CHAPTER 11

CREATIVE HUSTLE

There was a time in the 2010s when creatives were raising funds online in ways they had never done before. It was the golden age of crowdfunding and lots of artists who managed to gain support for projects large and small. Platforms like IndieGoGo, Kickstarter, and GoFundMe emerged as extremely popular methods for creatives. According to Wikipedia, "Crowdfunding is the practice of funding a project or venture by raising small amounts of money from a large number of people, in modern times typically via the Internet. Crowdfunding is a form of crowdsourcing and alternative finance." When crowdfunding first came out, people raised money for all sorts of creative projects. It was appealing to all types of people because it was a source of funding that didn't need to be paid back and offered total freedom for the beneficiary. Adventurous nomads used it to fund their travels. Entrepreneurs used it to start businesses. Inventors used to develop prototypes. Even celebrities like TLC utilized these platforms to fund anything from final album projects or to raising money for issues they were passionate about. Everyone was on it!

As time went on, though, scams popped up. Fraudulent causes were revealed in the news and media. There were many instances of misappropriation of funds. It got a bad reputation and people stopped trusting the campaigns. Now, crowdfunding is primarily used for crisis situations and most people are reluctant to donate money to anyone they don't know personally. People still use crowdfunding, however, now it is primarily reserved for medical bills, natural disaster relief efforts, and nonprofit organizations. Unfortunately, the crowdfunding bubble has burst, sending artists back to the drawing board as far as funding goes.

While most crowdfunding sites are unappealing to artists today, there are a few options that have taken over that spot in the creative space. Platforms like Patreon use the crowdsourcing model specifically to help creatives. This is a potential option, but note that it is most useful after you have already gotten your artistic career moving, have content to share, and have built a following. The whole concept is in the name which comes from the word, patron. Patrons have been around for centuries and are basically any individual offering support or funding to an artist or an organization.

Patreon works by setting up a monthly subscription service that your supports can join at different tier levels. They can support you for just one month or longer, and monthly payments can be as low as a few dollars or rise as high as thousands. Although Patreon is a viable option to maintain your creative career full-time, as we mentioned before, it works best for artists who already have an established audience. You'll also need to have plenty of content and services or products to reward your subscribers with. Like all of the options we've covered, there are pros and cons to utilizing the platform, so do your research before signing up to determine if this method will work for you.

Once you get the ball moving with your creative business, it's important to keep that momentum. You need to find ways of sustaining and maintaining your artistic career. Explore all of the ways you can potentially continue funding your work. Figure out exactly how others are making money doing what you are doing. Perhaps you will sell your art as a product or freelance your skills as a service. If you are good at teaching others you can even offer to educate others on your craft. This is another excellent place to get creative and find ways to expand your business. Keep in mind that marketing and promotion also play a role in these methods of maintaining your creative business. There is a skill to selling art on Etsy, attracting clients on Fiverr, or teaching classes on SkillShare. Learn the ins and outs of any platform you plan on utilizing. This is a great place to invest in yourself by enrolling in courses that will teach you more techniques of earning an income from your specific talent and how to have an impact online.

Remember what we said about going viral? While, statistically, it's like winning the lottery, there is actually more strategy involved in the digital space. Love him or hate him, Lil Nas X is a fascinating example of how you can play the game and win. Although it initially seemed that Lil Nas X was an overnight sensation, he worked hard and dedicated a large portion of his time studying exactly how to make something go viral. By utilizing social media strategy, he spent his time with trial and error across various platforms. This goes back to the importance of investing in the promotional side of your work. Lil Nas X may have done a lot of the marketing himself, but that meant less time to spend on his creative work. His ratio of time was divided similarly to what we recommend. He only spent 20-30 percent of his time working on his music. The rest of that 70-80 percent was used to learning what worked and what didn't work on Instagram, Twitter, and TikTok. Once he got his 15 minutes in the spotlight, he doubled down on the moment. He invested in elevating his career even higher. Now he is putting the money into the business side, which allows him even more time to be creative now. His team has spent millions getting him from where he was then to where he is now.

This goes back to hitting critical mass. Your work needs exposure to go far in the entertainment industry. Marketing is just the process of showing value to the consumer via mass exposure to your product. The verdict is out until you hit that critical mass. And you'll never know how good your art is until it gets to enough people. It's common for singers and bands to have old songs that aren't even listened to by audiences until their hit single comes out. Suddenly their following explodes and new fans are eager for more music. They consume an artist's entire catalog, searching for hidden gems and cult classics, consequentially causing tracks that have been out for years to jump to the top of the charts.

Even if you do have a project that goes viral, it will only take you so far. Eventually, you will have to invest in yourself to get to the top. Invest in things that will pay you back. Figure out everyplace you can make money with your art and utilize what works best for you. Maybe you can submit your songs for music licensing to be used in movies or television. We cannot stress this enough: you need to put yourself out there. Make sure all of your platforms are turned on for monetization and set up to pay you out. Sometimes this requires you to reach a certain following first, so follow any steps necessary to build your audience. If you are a performer of sorts, make sure that you are registered with a PRO, or a performing rights organization. These are steps you need to take to ensure you get paid for your work.

Artists in the music industry, for example, need to upload their music to every platform where music is being streamed. Many people will think of popular platforms like Spotify, but there are lots of other places people are listening to music, like Tidal, Deezer, and Apple Music. If you decide to invest in a promotional campaign, make sure you are paying legitimate companies dedicated to getting real streams. Most musicians, singers, and rappers earn their money from streams, so this is vital to your success in that industry. Like I always say, "If you ain't streaming, you're dreaming!"

Another thing to note, is most creatives, especially at the beginning of their career survive by diversifying their income streams. They might combine multiple methods of funding with a variety of techniques to draw a profit out of their creative business. Very few artists earn their full income from one method. There are so many benefits to diversifying your income, though. For one, it can act as a safety net in case one of your streams runs dry. For example, if you are only making money from your YouTube views, and your audience depends on new content to support you, this could put you in a tough position if you ever fail to upload a new video. This will give you more flexibility with your time too.

Whatever you do, you have to find a way to fund your creative business. It is crucial to find a way to finance the dream before the dream becomes a nightmare. The romanticized idea of the starving artist is all too appropriate for so many artists. I rarely see artists with good credit and a strong financial foundation. Most of them are struggling. Most of them are in debt. The few I've met who are well-off financially had to work hard for a long time to get where they are. Many of them learned the hard way by making mistakes. It took a great deal of patience and persistence for them to build their career up enough and figure out how the money worked. Some creatives never figure it out.

I know lots of creatives who are in debt. This is a common narrative for artists. We notice that the people in society who are financially stable have often gotten there by working in a specific way to reach that level. They have maintained stable jobs and maintained one income over long periods of time. Alternatively, creative individuals typically fail to excel in a corporate setting. They might go through lots of jobs in their lifetime, unsatisfied with any career that doesn't meet their artistic needs. Therefore, they struggle to keep a solid income. They resort to things like waiting tables on the side, working odd jobs, and only showing up part-time. It's a lot harder for them to set up a strong foundation to build from. If you are unable to consistently hold down a good-paying job, you're obviously going to struggle with paying bills on time and maintaining good credit. Living this way makes everything unstable. It isn't until they unlock the puzzle of turning their talent into a profitable business that they ever gain traction with their finances.

Most creatives could benefit greatly from having a business manager or financial advisor aiding them on their professional journey and making sure all of their ducks are in a row. An artist's mind works differently. Their strengths often are not based on the analytical side of things with numbers. They are loose and relaxed with money and struggle to keep their finances organized. We could chalk this all up to the right-brain vs. left-brain personality, and while some may be capable of tapping into both hemispheres, others will fail to tap into that skill set. The duality of being good with the creative side and with the financial side is a rarity. If you can unlock both of them, you will be unstoppable.

Even artists who attended school for their creative passion don't necessarily learn how to make money from the talent they studied so hard for. Arts degrees don't come with education on thriving in the real world. The focus is always on the craft, which only teaches you how to be a better writer, musician, or sculptor. This is great for building your creative skills, but you'll need a whole different skill set to survive as an artist. This all comes back to mindset. You have to be willing to invest both the time and money necessary to make it. Make it a point to learn business, marketing, and financial skills if you want to achieve the creative career of your dreams. Remember, you are the product, the brand, and the business. Change the lens so you can view it differently. Everything will start coming into focus.

"Your dream is your baby. It is your responsibility to usher it into the world."

CHAPTER 12

FINANCE THE DREAM

If you want to creatively enhance your business position, then it starts with understanding that you are both the business and the brand. This is the point we are driving home. This one piece of knowledge is enabling all types of artists everywhere to fully unlock creative finances. It all permeates from mindset. Perceiving yourself as a business and a brand is a mile marker and turning point on your creative voyage. When you can apply your creativity to the financial side of your work, you'll be able to put your ideas into action. Your dream is your baby and it is your responsibility to usher it into the world. There is no way around the elephant in the room. You have to find a way to finance your dream.

Out of all methods we've covered in this book, we still maintain that business credit is the best long-term solution to building and sustaining a creative brand. There are so many reasons why we love business credit so much. For one, a person's business will always be able to access three to four times more capital than an individual ever will. Many of the other options are one-and-done situations, or they tend to run out at some point. Family and friends will only support you for so long. They have a limit and it gets harder and harder to keep coming back asking for more money. Private investors will charge interest rates and have other stipulations while freelancing for clients takes valuable time away from your personal projects. Creative people like to have options and business credit gives artists the most possibilities. It also offers the most creative control and freedom. Another nail in the coffin.

As time goes on, you build credit, earning larger lines of funding. As long as you maintain good business credit it will just continue to get better and offer more and more. If executed properly, within a few years, your creative business could have access to hundreds of thousands of dollars! As long as you pay it back and build on it, it is always there and the lines just keep growing. It's something you can use for the rest of your career. It's a long game. Once your family gives you $25,000, are they going to give it to you again? What if the next project requires more and you need $50,000, are they going to give it to you then? On the other hand, if you use business credit for the $25,000 and you pay it back, you actually gain even more business credit. After it's established, business capital is always there. You aren't relying on anyone else to finance your dream. You can use it for whatever you need for your business. There are no rules on what you can and can't buy with business credit. You can use it for anything! Real estate, travel expenses, and equipment. Creatives like to get involved with other things and experiment. They might want to do more than just work on their craft. Maybe they aspire to start a record label or launch a clothing line.

Here's a story about a music group that was looking for help with funding: The four-man group had one member whose mother was helping support her son, but her finances were limited. She was running out of the means to keep the band afloat. When they came to me for advice, I encouraged them to take our course at World Capital Credit. They enrolled the next month. After learning about business credit, the mother was ecstatic. Everyone was relieved that she didn't have to pay for their studio time anymore. They ended up getting access to lines worth $30,000, which they used to launch their clothing line. They bought embroidery machines and screen printers. It allowed them to invest more into their creative business, ultimately enabling them to increase their earnings. With massive lines of credit, you can take ownership of your dream and control your own destiny.

Even seasoned veterans of the business world lack an understanding of business credit. Surprisingly, many entrepreneurs go their whole careers without taking the time to learn enough to utilize it. Some have a general idea of what it is, but they don't use it, and haven't built it. Building it is essential because it is not instant grits. It takes time to grow. The fastest timeline is between 6 months to a year or more for you to earn significant lines of credit. It might take even longer depending on where you're starting from and where you're trying to get to. This is something you need to commit to. Business credit certainly isn't the quickest route to funding. Handouts from the Friends and Family Plan can put money in your pocket immediately, but that has its limitations. Business credit is a long game. It takes dedication, patience, and deliberate action to build over time. But it can be a huge game-changer for people, which is why we are trying so hard to raise awareness about it in the creative community.

An old Chinese proverb says, "The best time to plant a tree is 20 years ago. The second-best time to plant a tree is today." Business credit is that tree. Plant it today and it will grow over time. As long as you use it responsibly, we promise you won't regret making this decision for your creative business. Even if you don't use it right away, it's a good failsafe and will be there for you later in your career if you want to expand.

Creatives need to get their head out of the clouds and awaken to the financial reality at hand. There's no way around it. To reiterate, if money is something you struggle with, make sure you put someone on your team who can handle the business dealings. Find a financial advisor you trust. Enlist professionals to back you up and keep you in check. Surround yourself with financially-minded people. Every celebrity and business mogul has people working with them to push their brand to the top. Invest in your business by hiring a rockstar team.

View your financial portfolio from the bigger picture. As a creative business, you'll need as many financial resources as are available. You can combine the methods we discussed here. For example, you can start with the Friends and Family Plan. With their support, you can launch your creative business and apply for credit. After building your career a bit, maybe you draw attention from a private investor. Utilize every option available to strengthen your entire financial portfolio. Creatives are always coming up with new ideas, as you grow as an artist, your projects will become more expensive. Set yourself up for success and solidify those resources for your future self. Your dream is your responsibility. You have to take ownership of it.

Many creatives hesitate to elevate their creative hobby to the professional level. If you aren't treating it like a business, it's just an expensive hobby. So, how do you know when you're ready to take the plunge and jump into using the financial options we covered? For starters, you need to have proof of concept. Creatives have lots of ideas that pull them in conflicting directions. Young girls come to me saying, "I can model, I can sing, I can act, I can rap… Oh and I dance too!" This is a classic jack of all trades and a master of none. A person like this will have to prove themselves across multiple concepts. Multi-talented creatives like Michael Jackson are rare. Get centered on what it is you want to be known for. Make sure you've done enough of whatever it is, that you are comfortable in your skin. Be 100 percent sure that this isn't just a phase for you, but something you will want to pursue long term. You must know beyond reasonable doubt that this is your gift. Notice how your audience reacts and responds to what it is you're doing. Other people need to be cosigning on the brand. This is the difference between having a creative business and an artistic hobby.

Once you get to a point where you aren't just tinkering anymore and you know that you can do this thing for real, you can start building. Eventually, creatives reach a moment in their career where they wonder about quitting their day job so they can devote themselves completely to the art. Be absolutely certain that what you are creating is a viable brand. If you can monetize your creative career into one-third or half of what you're making at your full-time job, then you're ready for that leap of faith. There needs to be equity and financial appeal before you are ready to go pro. I always tell my clients, "An artist must be viable, monetizable, and scalable in order to be investable."

It really just depends on what floor you want to jump from. Some people are maniacs and will jump headfirst from the top floor. They frantically try to open a financial parachute as they fall. Others are more cautious. They want to fully replace their income before they jump and wait until the art is making exactly what they were earning in their 9-5 position. Whenever you finally take that leap of faith, it will give you extra time to work on your creative business. It's a real quagmire. The money has to catch up to your vision before the rubber meets the road. You're in a war and you're going to have to find a way to win. The methods in this book are here to help you.

The COVID-19 pandemic shifted the workforce around in 2020, resulting in a labor movement many are calling "The Great Resignation." Everyone is demanding more satisfying work. They are becoming their own boss and setting their own hours. People everywhere are stepping out of their comfort zones and seizing the opportunity to finally answer their true calling. Countless people all over the world are soul searching, asking themselves what it is they really want to do. Figuring it out is not easy, but it's critical to find more fulfilling work. Get clear on where you are going and start taking the steps to get there.

As you continue from here on your creative journey, beware the dream stealers. Stay away from anyone who says, "you'll never be able to do that." Or, "you can't afford it." There will always be doubters out there. Sometimes it's not even that they doubt you, but instead, they doubt the whole industry. They aren't looking for reasons why you can win, they only see how you will fail. Don't let their energy bring you down.

And don't tell yourself these things either. Stop that train of thought before it even leaves the station! Any time you say, "No, I can't," you are programming your brain with a limiting belief system. The possibilities of what you are capable of are endless. Instead, respond to doubt by asking, "How?" For example, if you catch yourself saying, "I can't afford to do that." Tweak it. Make it a question. "HOW will I afford to do that?"

Humans are great at problem-solving. Our brains are perfectly designed to figure things out. Saying "can't" creates a barrier in your mind. As far as your subconscious is concerned, it isn't a question to be answered, but an established fact. But when you twist that around, it becomes a puzzle to solve. Take a moment right now to ask yourself this question, "How will I build my creative career?"

What looks impossible is actually possible. You CAN find a way to finance your dream. You don't need to feel hopeless or helpless. Never let those negative thoughts stop you in your tracks. Give your brain permission to find the solution. You can do this! You just have to find a way.

If you're still uncertain about taking that next step, have a little faith in yourself. This is your purpose, after all. It's hard to walk through the next door if you are still holding another door open. You have to let the last door close before you can walk through the next one. You are sitting on the threshold of creative financing. It's time to open the door of possibilities and shut the door on your money troubles once and for all.

"The best time to plant a tree is 20 years ago. The second-best time to plant a tree is today."

-Chinese Proverb

BONUS CHAPTER 13

THE 9 MOST DEVASTATING MISTAKES

The 9 Most Devastating Mistakes Entrepreneurs & Business Owners Make When Financing Their Businesses ... and How to Avoid Them

Devastating Mistake #9 Using Personal Credit to Finance Your Business

This is the hands-down biggest and most common mistake entrepreneurs make. It is using personal credit to finance their businesses. Common examples include:

- Paying for business expenses with your personal credit cards
- Taking out personal loans to finance your business expenses

If you've used one or more of these financing methods to fund your entrepreneurial ventures, I'm not surprised. Shockingly, many business startup experts recommend these methods for funding new businesses. This advice is meant well. But it is still dangerous. The reason for not using your personal credit for business purposes is simple: You WILL destroy your personal credit. It's inevitable.

By using your valuable personal credit for business expenses, you run the risk of:

- Lowering your personal credit score. When you personally guarantee business-related financing, the lender will want a personal credit check. With every inquiry into your credit history, your personal credit score takes a hit. The lower your score drops, the harder it is to get financing, especially financing with the most favorable terms.

- Reducing the amount of credit available for personal use. The more credit you have personally guaranteed for your business, the higher your debt-to-income ratio soars. And if you need loans for personal use, you will get less from lenders. Signing a loan for your business could keep you from getting a mortgage on the new house you plan to buy a year from now.

- Losing everything. When you use your personal resources or credit to finance a business, you chain your financial security to your company's success. If the company fails, you are be left holding the bag. And your personal finances will sink along with your business. You'll never recoup the 'loan' you took from your retirement account to get your business launched. Creditors will be calling you for payment. And if things get bad enough, you may have to declare bankruptcy.

To protect your financial security, don't use your personal credit to finance your business activities. Instead, secure credit in your company's name. You do not have to risk your personal assets or lower your personal credit score. And you will eventually be able to get credit without a personal guarantee.

Devastating Mistake #8 Putting Personal Assets at Risk

Each time you pledge personal assets for any type of credit for your business, you jeopardize your personal belongings. These include savings and investment accounts, your car, and even your home. If your business can't pay off its debt, the bank will come looking for you to make good on the loan. A sole proprietorship is most susceptible to this risk. You can build business credit as a sole proprietor. But you will be completely liable for all personal and corporate debt. Your credit history only comes from activity associated with your social security number. This is because you will not have a corporate tax ID number. As a sole proprietor, you also have no legal means to separate corporate and personal credit.

The best way to protect your personal assets is to incorporate your business. You'll shield yourself from personal liability for the company's debts and often will also reduce your tax burden.

Devastating Mistake #7 Contaminating Your Credit

When people marry, they vow to share their lives. For some good-hearted but financially naïve couples, this means sharing personal credit.

Unfortunately, adding your spouse to your credit isn't a show of undying loyalty and devotion. It's credit file contamination – an almost unforgivable sin if you're a business owner.

When you initiate joint credit, your spouse's credit history becomes part of your credit file. If your spouse misses a payment, the delinquency affects your credit. The matter is complicated further if you haven't separated personal credit from company credit. Credit file contamination from a spouse's credit history could keep you from achieving business goals. Because it will keep you from securing the financing necessary to grow your company.

Avoid credit file contamination. Keep your credit history completely separate from your spouse's. If your spouse ruins their credit, then you'll still have a good credit history to support your family and business.

Devastating Mistake #6 Not Paying Your Bills on Time, 100% of the Time

You misplaced your credit card bill and sent in payment a few days late. It happens to the best of us, right? Maybe so. But as an entrepreneur, you can't afford even a single late payment, whether business or personal. Your credit file is a complete history of your credit activity. Not paying your bills on time can ruin your credit file. A single delinquency can be held against you for years and be used to prevent extending existing credit or denying new credit. And this can make or break your ability to finance the launch, operation, or growth of your company.

There are two ways to protect yourself from this critical mistake. The first, obviously, is to make sure to pay your bills on time. Second, keep your personal credit separate from your corporate credit. That way, problems with personal credit history will not affect corporate credit. But if you fail to separate your corporate and personal credit, problems with your personal credit file could directly affect your ability to build your corporate credit and your business.

Devastating Mistake #5 Using Your Family's Money

When you use a personal credit card for business, you instantly slash your amount of credit available. This is your personal credit to get what you and your family need and want. Many Americans see credit cards as a financial cushion to carry them through emergencies. This includes an illness making it impossible to work. Hence wasting your credit on business expenses weakens your safety net. Still, many entrepreneurs ignore the dramatic consequences of this dangerous practice:

- They buy business-related items with their personal credit cards hoping to pay themselves back one day.

- They get other personal credit cards, leases, loans and lines of credit and then use them for business expenses. Once they exhaust their borrowing limits, they persuade family members to use their credit to keep the business afloat.

Be forewarned. If you convince your family to finance your business, you're just digging a deeper hole for them to crawl out of. If your business fails, it could wipe out your family financially. This is as 95% of business do in the first five years, according to the Small Business Administration. Don't ask family members to use their personal credit to invest in your business.

As we discussed in Mistake #9, using your personal credit for business expenses is a strategic error. And if it doesn't make sense for you, the business owner, it makes even less sense for family members. Keep everyone's personal credit strictly separate from your company's corporate credit.

Devastating Mistake #4 Not Incorporating and Building Corporate Credit the Right Way

Many business owners are unaware of the value of incorporation. Even fewer understand the essential steps necessary to build corporate credit. This is credit where they can take full advantage of their entrepreneurial status. Incorporation makes your business entity separate from you, the business owner. The business becomes a separate entity with its own liability.

Incorporation separates your business assets from your personal assets. If sues your company, they cannot touch your house, car, or anything else owned by you or your family. But removing personal liability for company debts and actions isn't the only reason to incorporate.

Let's face it. You are in business to make money. To make a profit and sustain your business, you need capital – in the right place, at the right time – to help your business grow. By incorporating your business, your business can start establishing corporate credit. This will ultimately provide the funds you need to grow your business. And you can one day get to the point where your business can get funding without a personal guarantee. Keep in mind, this takes time to do. But incorporating doesn't automatically qualify you for all the corporate credit you need. And it does not qualify you for the best type of corporate credit. Your goal should be to secure cash. This is not lines of credit tied to particular stores or vendors. It should be where you do not need to offer a personal guarantee. To secure this "Holy Grail" of corporate credit, you must follow a well-defined, step-by-step system. This is to build your corporate credit history and business credit score.

Some of preliminary steps to excellent corporate credit include incorporating and maintaining a physical office. They also include getting a local phone number and a 411 listing. And get a business license and have a business with real revenue. These steps pave the way for building your credit score with business credit bureaus. Follow those preliminary steps and provide the bureaus with the information they want. Then you will be ready to approach the few lenders who will give you a cash line of credit with no personal guarantee. These are a few lenders which will help you keep your business and personal assets separate. And they will give you the cash you need to grow your business.

Devastating Mistake #3 Rushing the Process For Building Corporate Credit

Corporate credit can be an invaluable tool as you build your wealth. This is because it gives you the flexibility to invest money to help build your business. It takes time and patience to build wealth. And it also takes time and patience to build corporate credit to get cash from lenders with no personal guarantee. Incorporating your business is just the start of the process. You can build corporate credit to where you can get cash without a personal guarantee. The industry standard says this takes two to three years.

Devastating Mistake #2 Not Following Up on the Credit Building Process

Once they start following the prescribed process for building corporate credit, many entrepreneurs simply don't do enough follow-up work. But if you don't keep track of your progress while building excellent corporate credit, you may miss key elements. These could make the difference between getting the cash line of credit you need, or getting a denial.

It is always a good idea to delegate, especially if you are busy. But you have to be careful about which kind of work you delegate. Work that directly affects the growth of your business and your wealth deserves your personal attention.

Devastating Mistake #1 Not Recognizing Opportunity Costs

At the first sign of profits or the first influx of credit, many business owners spend on material goods. This can be more than they have – or even more than they will make. Lured by the luxury car or exotic vacation they've lusted after for years, they ignore long-term business goals. Instead, they go for temporary and immediate gratification. But if you want to achieve your long-term business goals, you cannot do this. Instead, only leverage corporate credit and profits to create greater gains for your business. Don't try to figure out how much profit you can take out of the business. Instead, learn how to invest earnings to deliver greater returns for your business.

This is not, by any means, a comprehensive list of all the mistakes entrepreneurs make when building corporate credit. But if you address these costly and dangerous errors, you will be on your way to building a safe, secure, and financially sound business. It can be the business you always dreamed of!

"We manage the dream. We don't finance it." -Rob Terell

BONUS CHAPTER 14

VITAL QUESTIONS YOU MUST ASK BUSINESS CREDIT BUILDING COMPANIES!

So many people who hire business credit building companies are unhappy with the results. Before choosing another company, ask these questions. Then you can be assured it is a legitimate company that can help you build business credit. Why is it so important to work with knowledgeable advisors? Why can't you do it on your own? The Fair Credit Reporting Act does not apply to the business credit bureaus. This means if you make a mistake, skip a step, or try and take a shortcut, your business credit file can be red-flagged. This means your company is prohibited from receiving credit. There is a proven step-by-step process you MUST follow if you plan on properly building your business credit. If you don't follow the proven process then you can be put into the High-risk category. If this happens, no lending institution will lend your business money and there is nothing you can do to remove it. Make sure to choose an honest credit building company with the knowledge, experience and proven systems to support you.

Vital Questions You Must Ask Before Working With Any Business Credit Building Company!

Before you decide which company to work with, make sure to ask them these 5 vital questions.

Question #1: Will I Get Only Trade Credit or Cash Credit? Be careful, there are a number of companies which only help you get trade credit. You can only use trade credit with the individual creditor, and nowhere else. This is great if you need $3,000 of paper products. But is useless if you need money to invest, cover business expenses or expand your company. But for CASH credit, do you always have to personally guarantee the application? If the company claims you must always personally guarantee all types of credit, you are NOT receiving the full benefit of business credit. Keep in mind, our solution introduces you to lenders who do not require a personal guarantee. But these vendors still check your personal credit and need your Social Security Number. They do this to stay in banking compliance.

Question #2: Will a Trained Coach Show Me, Step by Step, How to Incorporate my Business and Build Business Credit? My guess is if you wanted to figure out the intricacies of Incorporating your business, and building corporate credit on your own, you would already done so. I've done it. And believe me – this is NOT stuff you want to muddle through on your own. So, if you won't get step by step instructions supported by a trained credit coach, resulting in a predicable successful outcome, call another company. We spell out each step in our proven system for revolving credit cards without a personal guarantee. And we do it in crystal clear detail.

Question #3: If I Get Stuck While Taking All Those Necessary Steps, Do I Have to Pay You Hundreds or Even Thousands to Help me Figure it Out? Many companies charge low fees up front and then tack on heavy, additional charges each time you call or write for help. Not us! We deliver everything you need to know to get business credit without a personal guarantee. You have access to a dedicated coaching advisor. There are no limits on how often you can speak with them.

Question #4: When it Comes Time to Apply for Financing, Are You Going to Pass Me Off from Lender to Lender? This is another very important question. Virtually every other credit building will, when it is time to apply for financing, pass you off to one lender to apply. And they will then tell you to apply at the next lender and so on. They send you on a wild goose chase and hope one of the lenders can get financing for you. Does this sound like something a real business credit and financing expert would do? We don't! In fact, we are the ONLY company with multiple business lending programs programmed into our Business Credit Builder. We know each lender's underwriting criteria. Finance officers pre-qualify based off of the clients need and access where to send the file to. Sometimes you're reviewed by multiple lenders in order to get the best rate, term possible. Once a client provides their credit report to us, we will review it with them and advise if they are ready to move to the next Step/Tier and go over accounts in that Step/Tier. Then we direct you to view the Learn more section and apply yourself with that vendor account.

Question #5: What Kind of a Guarantee Do You Offer? It's critical to get the specifics about guarantees. This is because most companies offering guarantees only promise an 80+ PAYDEX score for your corporation. While this is a start, it's not good enough.

If you address these costly and dangerous errors, you will be on your way to building a safe, secure, and financially sound business—the business you always dreamed of!

ACKNOWLEDGMENTS

First, thanks to almighty God, the most high for blessing me with all of my gifts, talents, and abilities to do what I do. All honor, glory, and praise to you! God is amazing! Special thanks to my family, true friends, business colleagues, and supporters who hold me down every day, and have always been there for me to celebrate the wins and help me get through the "L's". You guys are my heroes! To my writing partner, Lydia Plantamura, you're a special and gifted writer, couldn't have pulled this off without you girllll. Thanks a million, and I hope that's what we make!

The whole Wealth Nation, Industry Certified, Musicnomics, and Live Legendary teams, we do it for the culture, not for the money. Hopefully, this book inspires a forward-thinking culture and helps some good talented people make a lot of money in this business.